LIFE
— IN THE —
SLOW
LANE

I Live in a Nursing Home and I Like It

Jean Misura

McKinnon Books

Editor: Kelli Sallman
Cover design: Brett Grimes Design
Interior Design and Typesetting: Draft2Digital

Library of Congress Cataloging-in-Publication Data
Publisher's Cataloging-In-Publication Data
(Prepared by The Donohue Group, Inc.)

Names: Misura, Jean.
Title: Life in the slow lane : I live in a nursing home and I like it / Jean
Misura.
Description: Dallas, Texas : McKinnon Books, [2016]
Identifiers: LCCN 2016912645 | ISBN 978-0-9977878-0-1 | ISBN
    978-0-9977878-1-8 (ebook)
Subjects: LCSH: Misura, Jean. | Nursing home patients--Anecdotes. |
Nursing homes--Anecdotes. | Older people--Care--Anecdotes. | Older
people--Dignity--Anecdotes.
Classification: LCC RC954.3 .M57 2016 (print) | LCC RC954.3 (ebook) |
DDC 362.16--dc23

Contents

Chronology

Fall 1960   – Experiences first onset of multiple sclerosis at
               age forty
Fall 1967   – Receives official MS diagnosis
July 1970   – Needs cane
Sept. 1971 – Needs wheelchair
July 1976   – Confined by gallbladder surgery to hospital bed
May 1977   – Youngest daughter earns degree and leaves home
Nov. 1981 – Begins herbal and nutritional regimen
Feb. 1982   – Divorces Rudy
Mar. 1982 – Enters County Home and Infirmary
Aug. 1982 – Enters Amherst Nursing Home (now Elderwood
               Health Care) at age sixty-two
Jan. 1985   – Daughter dies.
Dec. 1995 – Begins journaling
Apr. 1997   – Husband dies
Nov. 2008 – Dies from natural causes.

Prologue

I HAVE SPENT the past thirteen years in a nursing home.

In the fall of 1960, multiple sclerosis (MS) began its assault on my lifestyle. I was forty years old. Loss of peripheral vision in my left eye was the first indication that something was wrong. The ophthalmologist said, "Go to your family doctor to see if he can find what's causing it." He couldn't. Six years later I went to an internist even though his fee was high. I needed a good diagnostician because my symptoms of weakness and fatigue had become so severe that they could no longer be ignored. Between the internist and a neurologist it was decided I had a demyelinating disease, their euphemism for this invasion that changes the lives of one's whole family. My internist described the disease but never used the words *multiple sclerosis*. For this I would always be grateful. It removed much of the trauma from the revelation of this dreaded diagnosis.

A demyelinating disease is a disease of the central nervous system. A myelin sheath encases the spinal cord similar to the way insulation protects an electrical cord. Something erodes the myelin in apparently random attacks. This erosion interrupts communication from the brain to whichever area is controlled by the site of the erosion. The involved body parts depend on where along the spinal cord the attacks occur. My legs don't move because, even though my brain is sending out the command, my legs don't receive it. My left arm is also affected. But I am lucky that the MS hasn't affected my speech as it does in some.

The internist recommended taking Lipoflavonoid, a dietary supplement combining vitamin C and some of the B vitamins. He said this sometimes helped if the problem is caught soon enough. Apparently, it wasn't caught soon enough. I began to suspect that I had MS. When I asked the doctor during my annual physical a year later, he admitted that's what it was. By this time I had had it for seven years, so my attitude was, "So what else is new," which was a false air of stoicism. I think I infused myself with an emotional numbness.

The etiology of MS is still uncertain. Some in the medical community believe that it is a virus that attacks the myelin. Others think that it is an autoimmune disease where the body's immune system goes berserk and attacks its own body protein. I tend to agree with the latter theory. Don't know why. Gut instinct, I guess. Incidentally, there's a very high incidence of MS in the Great Lakes region. No one knows how or why this is so.

I was luckier than some. I already had had my family. My daughter Nancy was twenty-three by the time I found out that my diagnosis was multiple sclerosis, seven years after the onset. She was living in Florida. Kathy was eighteen, Susan sixteen, and Peggy twelve. Shortly after the diagnosis, I became a wall-walker, using the furniture and walls to balance myself. I could still handle grocery shopping by using the outside wall of the house and the outside of the car to aid my entrance into the car. The grocery cart supported my supermarket rounds.

In the summer of '70 I had to face the fact that my disease was progressing. By July I could no longer put off purchasing a cane. I went from cane to walker to wheelchair in fourteen months. My diagnosis may not have been traumatic but my descent into a wheelchair was. I sobbed and sobbed in helplessness. To never be able to walk again! This wasn't real. It was a nightmare.

In July of 1976 I had to have my gall bladder removed. By Christmastime of that year, I realized that the hospital bed we had rented as a temporary convenience during my convalescence would be a continuing necessity. This was one step further into the loss of independence. But nobody ever promised me a rose garden, and it was a damn good thing. Because I sure wasn't getting one.

In 1977 our youngest daughter Peggy graduated with an Associates Degree in radiation therapy and left for her first job treating cancer patients at a hospital one and a half hours from home. Our proximity to a university enabled us to hire students to help transfer me from bed to wheelchair to toilet and back as well as do some cooking and laundry in exchange for room and board. This worked out well for the next four years.

But my condition continued deteriorating, and I eventually realized it was becoming more difficult for just one person to transfer me. I was becoming weaker and less able to put any energy into the transfers. It was also an unpleasant atmosphere in which to try to maintain a normal family life.

Whether I was or not, I felt I was an irritant to my other family household members, which by this time was only my husband. I wasn't sick. I looked healthy. I had a good appetite. I didn't complain. I appeared to be content with having to have all my needs fulfilled by someone else. I wasn't as content as I appeared to be, but I didn't do a lot of complaining about my lot in life.

My husband Rudy had his own business, which made more demands on him than a nine-to-five job would have. He was a furrier—not a fur merchant—a true furrier. He made garments out of fur collars and other used but still good pieces of fur. He thus was able to sell them more cheaply than furriers who sold new garments.

When he came home after work, instead of having a wife who had dinner ready and a comforting embrace, he found a wife who needed to be waited on. Our marriage had not been a smooth one for many years. Rudy was paranoid, which made him difficult to live with. Both of us were stubborn. What little patience he had gradually eroded, and I felt he would be happier if he were free to make a life for himself. And I would be happier in a friendlier environment, among professionals who were paid to cope with problems like mine.

After a long emotional struggle, I decided to divorce him and move into a nursing home. He was reluctant. I think he felt the stigma of divorce more keenly than me. But I was adamant. Kathy was married and had her own family by this time. Sue had her own apartment. Nancy and Peggy lived out of state.

My children, my niece Judy, and her husband Don had been seeing an iridologist named Adele. She dealt in herbal healing. She treated no specific illness. She looked into the body through the eye, illuminated by a small light, and pinpointed the trouble spots. Her recommendations were designed to get rid of these trouble spots and to restore balance. Adele knew of my plight through my kids and Judy and Don. In November of '81 she told Don, "Tell Jean not to go into a nursing home until she sees me."

He made an appointment for me immediately, and a few weeks later my doctor's secretary took me to the Catholic high school where Adele saw clients once a week. Because of the difficulty in transferring me, Adele did her viewing in the car.

My program included twenty-seven different vitamins and herbs (dandelion, alfalfa, licorice root, sarsaparilla, slippery elm, horsetail, comfrey, fenugreek, and others) in capsule or pill form one, two, or three times a day; several specific herb teas; and two drinks—one containing black cherry juice and a raw egg and the other containing a bunch of things including capsicum to make it spicy hot. There were many dietary restrictions—no sugar, coffee, tea, wheat flour, or citrus fruit (unless tree ripened). No nuts except in butter form, no red meat, and no tomatoes, green peppers, or eggplant. She recommended eating a lot of brown rice, lentils, yellow cornmeal, and parsley as well as eating fresh garlic and fresh ginger root three times per day, four vegetables with each meal, and four fresh fruits per day.

Assimilating all this was an exhausting schedule, but in a situation like mine you feel better trying something than doing nothing. I started the regimen that November.

Spontaneous remissions are not uncommon in cases of multiple sclerosis, but neither are they common. For twenty-one years I had been going steadily downhill, but starting that November, I found I no longer got worse. The program Adele put me on apparently stopped the progression of my disease. In spite of the skeptics I have encountered, I feel that a spontaneous remission at that exact time would have been too coincidental to be likely.

But the twenty-one years of steady decline still left me in need of professional care. Checking out nursing homes, I found out from my MS society counselor that our County Home and Infirmary had some young residents, so that was my first choice. I thought young residents would be more on the ball than older ones, more interesting to talk to.

I entered County Home in March of '82 and left five days later. When they found out about my herbal program, they almost had collective apoplexy. They were afraid other residents might get into my pills. The medical director and the director of nursing met with me to discuss this creature who had put me on such an outlandish program.

"Who is this woman?" the director of nursing asked. "Does she have a degree?"

To this day I'm sorry I didn't reply, "You have a degree, don't you? What can you do to help me?"

I went back home and started over. This time I told the nursing homes about my pills in advance. No one was willing to take me except Amherst Nursing Home where my personal physician, Dr. John Wayland, was the medical director. Douglas Castallana, the administrator, said he would take me if I kept my pills locked up. So on August 4, 1982, with outward bravado and inward tremors, I moved into my new home. The social worker, whose job it was to greet me, was on vacation, so Mr. Castallana (hereafter known as Doug or Mr. C.) ushered me in. He was forty-seven years old, over six feet tall, dark-and-Italian good looking, and slightly bald on top in the way many women consider sexy. He had a charming Boston accent. I was to learn that when he donned a fedora and put a cigar in his mouth, he looked like a 1930s gangster. He welcomed me with a casual warmth that eliminated some of my apprehension.

Amherst Nursing Home (now known as Elderwood Health Care at Wedgewood) is a small facility—eighty-three beds. Therein lies its charm. We're more like a family than the larger facilities. It has two wings. The south wing runs off the lobby in an arc to the right and the north wing runs off the lobby in an arc to the left. The physical therapy room is straight back from the lobby. The kitchen is off a short hallway to the left of the lobby. The dining room is also to the left of the lobby behind the kitchen, and the activities room is behind the dining room. There are three offices off the lobby, which also contains the reception area. Other offices are on the wings and in the basement, and that's it.

I was assigned to room number six, a two-bed room on the south wing. I soon became accustomed to my new home mainly because of people like Lucinda who lived across the hall from me. She taught my roommate and me a bunch of dirty words and expressions in Italian. It was fun and shocking to some of the more dignified Italians.

She had an endearing way of expressing herself. Instead of telling her daughter she was getting too fat, she said to her, "Did you eat breakfast this morning? If I was you, I wouldn't have." She died twelve years ago, and I still miss her.

The dietary staff was wonderful about cooperating with me on my dietary needs for Adele's regimen. I bought some of my own food, and they kept it in a special basket in the walk-in refrigerator. After a few years I started cheating—sometimes by eating beef, sometimes cheese, sometimes candy or other sweets and coffee. But by then, the benefits of the regimen seemed to have taken hold, and the deteriorating process had stopped.

After I was here a few months someone asked, "Do you play pinochle? A seat is available."

Well, I do. I love cards, and now I was in a position to indulge this favorite recreation. Wow! I thought. This would be like an ongoing vacation.

My elation was short-lived.

A nursing home pinochle game is not like an afternoon with the boys in the corner saloon. It goes something like this:

Dwight is at my left. He's tall and thin with angular features, probably in his late seventies and seems to be in good health. He's been volunteering here for several years. Emma's my partner. She's a sweet, plump, little Italian grandmother. Her gray hair is pulled back in a bun, and her brown doe eyes reflect her gentleness. Everyone loves her. Mattie's at my right. Mattie has soft features and gray eyes beneath a head full of short, neatly coiffed, black hair, courtesy Ms. Clairol. She wears thick glasses. She has beautiful clothes and costume jewelry, and she always wears makeup.

Mattie faces life bravely despite her tragic background. Her only child, a handsome son, and her husband both died unexpectedly. A hit-and-run driver killed her son right after he had been accepted into pre-med school. Her husband died on the operating table while having minor surgery for a hernia.

I suspect that both Mattie and Emma were once sharp card players, but they are both in their eighties, and, though they are far from the dementia class, time has taken its share of brain cells. Mattie deals. I'm suspicious. I count my cards. I have eleven.

I say, "I'm one short."

Everybody counts their cards. Dwight and Emma have eleven, Mattie has fifteen. We each draw one from Mattie.

Emma says, "What's trump?"

I say, "We don't know yet. I bid twenty-one."

Dwight says, "What's trump?"

I say, "Do you pass?"

He says yes, his voice showing annoyance that I'm asking a stupid question.

Emma says, "Pass," in answer to my question.

Mattie says, "What's trump?"

I assume that means she passes, so I lay down my run in spades and a marriage in diamonds.

Emma says, "What's trump?"

I tell her, "Spades."

She can't find any meld. That doesn't mean she doesn't have any.

"We have seventeen," I say.

They have eight. Dwight marks it down. I lead the ace of spades.

"What's trump?" Mattie asks.

"That is," I say.

Everybody follows suit. I lead the ace of diamonds, then the queen. Mattie throws a club.

"Don't you have any more diamonds?" I ask.

"If I did, I'd play one," she snaps.

"Don't you have any trump?" I venture meekly.

"What's trump?" she says.

"Spades," I answer.

"Oh, sure," she says and exchanges the club for a spade.

I tell her, "Take the trick. It's yours."

She leads the ace of clubs. Everybody follows suit. Next comes the queen of clubs. Emma trumps it.

"Don't you have any clubs?" I say.

"No," she assures me.

She leads her two aces of hearts, then the jack of clubs.

I have low blood pressure. This event brings it up close to normal—fringe benefit.

"You reneged three tricks ago." My voice was eight decibels higher than is socially acceptable. "You trumped a club when you had a club."

"What's trump?" she asks.

I try to keep my voice low, controlled so as not to further upset the equilibrium of my psyche. Spades, I answer in my new voice.

Having found the trick in question, I spread the cards to show her. I make her exchange the jack of clubs for her trump and give the trick to our opponents. I give the lead to Mattie since it should have been her lead three tricks ago. She leads the ace of trump. Dwight throws an off card. I take the next trick and lead my ten of spades.

Everybody throws an off card.

"There's a trump out yet," I say.

"What's trump?" Mattie asks.

"Spades," I say. "Somebody's got a spade yet."

They search their hands. Three heads shake no.

"C'mon, somebody's got a trump," I insist, accusingly.

Three heads are still going no. Mattie looks in Emma's hand. "There it is," she says. Emma takes back her discard and exchanges it for the trump. The hand continues. I lead my last card.

"Is that trump?" asks Mattie.

This is just a one-morning-a-week-affair, so I figure I can handle that much. Dwight comes in only once a week.

The following week we start the game with Mattie dealing. Mattie always holds up the deck of cards facing her partner as she deals so all of us can see the cards as she peels them off the deck. I keep my eyes averted because I don't need an unfair advantage, and the others don't even notice. In the middle of the first hand, Mattie plays her ten of diamonds on Dwight's jack and my queen. Emma plays the ace. Mattie takes her ten back and plays the jack.

I say, "You can't do that."

Mattie is the haughtiest wheelchair inhabitant I've met so far, and she manages to ignore a person with a contempt that squelches all argument. Two tricks later she reneges.

When I point it out she snaps, "I did not."

I find the trick and show her. Without a word she exchanges it for the proper card, and we continue the game.

It's getting near lunchtime, and we have time, maybe, for one more hand. It starts out okay. Halfway through the hand Mattie lays down a queen of spades and jack of diamonds for meld. Dwight adds four to their score. I let it pass. I'm not about to get into a discourse on the illegality of late meld with a woman who can slay me with one look. We play a few more tricks, and then Emma leads the ace of trump (hearts). This would ordinarily be okay, but this is the third time the ace of hearts has been played.

I abandon my new voice. I'm approaching screaming. "Where did you get that?"

"Why, in my hand," she says, puzzled that I should be upset.

I glance at everybody's hands. We all have four cards; Emma has eight. Without my noticing it, she has taken a trick and put it in her hand instead of on the table in front of her.

"I think lunch is ready," I yell, and throw my cards in.

Three days later another pinochle player entered the home, and I relinquished my seat to her. I'm not ready for the major leagues yet.

In December 1995, I began writing a journal about my life here and what I have learned about the human condition. By sharing my experiences with readers outside the nursing home, I hoped to communicate the joy and laughter, along with the sadness, that occur on a regular basis in a setting that many people view as depressing and without any redeeming characteristics. I had no idea then what lay ahead, or how the connections I had made at Elderwood would give me life when all I could see was death.

1

You Were Crazy before You Got Here

December 3, 1995

HERB AND SOPHIA came over to play pinochle today. Herb's
wife used to be a resident in this nursing home. She died about
six years ago, and he has always remained in touch. He, his
wife, Sophia, and her husband were friendly when all four were
alive, so Herb and Sophia just drifted together after their
spouses died, first as friends, then as lovers. They're a fun
couple. Sophia is always my partner. She is pleasant to look at.
Her gray hair is speckled with brown. Her off-the-face hairdo
exposes her round face still sprinkled with freckles, which
contribute to making her look younger than her seventy-four
years. Herb, who is in his mid-seventies, resembles Gary
Cooper, except he's not as tall and he's more talkative (Sophia
would say mouthy). Herb includes me in his playful insults,
and we do as much laughing as playing pinochle.

Sophia told me about her girlfriend who had a stroke
recently and was paralyzed on her left side. Sophia was at her
friend's house yesterday. She had to stay with her while her
friend's husband did some errands. When Sophia was leaving,
the husband accompanied her to her car.

He said, "I don't know what I'm going to do. I can't
handle this. I'd have to take off my socks to count the number
of times I had to take her to the bathroom yesterday. I don't

know how much longer I can last, but she made me promise I'd never put her in a nursing home."

That's when I decided to write this book.

I don't know what people who dread the idea of coming to a nursing home think we are doing here. We're having a ball is what we're doing—those of us who have all our marbles and who aren't wallowing in resentment at having been "put" here. We are not interested in giving our families guilt trips to punish them. We want more to acknowledge our situation and to figure out how to accommodate ourselves to it.

I think we have a terrific Activities Department in this nursing home even though I have nothing to compare it to. We play trivia, Scrabble, and do crossword puzzles and word games for the mind. We have bingo, bottoms up, jackpot, and Pokeno to satisfy the gambling spirit. We have basketball, bowling (limited of course), and other ball-throwing games for exercise. We do crafts.

We allot an hour each morning when the lowest functioning group can enjoy rocking dolls and stuffed animals in a private setting. And they do enjoy it. They're read to and sung to on a one-to-one basis.

There's participatory baking twice a week and a "celebrity chef" luncheon once a month. Six residents at a time are invited to participate in the preparation of the special luncheon—hosted by an individual on the staff or a family member—and then enjoy the fruits of their labors. There are movies a few times each month. There are wrestling afternoons for the men. They watch wrestling while drinking beer and eating junk food in a room by themselves.

We have parties on many occasions including Presidents' Day and Martin Luther King Jr. Day. We have outside entertainment frequently. Some of it is volunteered, and some we pay for. The Catholic Alumni Club band has been volunteering its talents every month for twenty-some years, and we look forward to every appearance eagerly. Live music is a treat here the same as it is out in the real world. We were presented with a karaoke machine, anonymously, and it provides a lot of hilarity. I seldom participate in the scheduled activities anymore because I'm busy with my computer, or pinochle, or reading detective or lawyer novels. But those who appreciate being in a position of utter retirement, with no pressing responsibilities, do enjoy the activities.

I think it's thoughtless when a spouse or parent imposes a promise to "never put me in a nursing home," with all its potential hardships, on those they love. Nursing homes today still carry some of the stigma of the nursing homes of yesterday, and it's a shame. My partner at pinochle today was Mildred, who is paralyzed on the left side from a stroke. I asked her if she was happier here than with her son who worked all day.

She said, "Oh, gosh, yes. There was nothing to do there except watch television."

I feel the same way. When I was home I was in a hospital bed in the living room, alone all day until five o'clock. I watched soap operas and napped, talked on the telephone, napped, knitted, napped, made potholders and napped. The excitement couldn't have entertained a dust bunny.

When I decided to enter a nursing home, I knew there would be no one but old people to associate with—I was only sixty-two—but I'm a realist. I figured what had to be had to be. What I hadn't taken into account were the nurses, aides, clerical staff, maintenance staff, and dietary staff. A nursing home is full of youth. There's more staff than residents, so the balance is in favor of youth. Since I hear all about their family problems and financial problems and, most interesting of all, their romantic problems, I feel right in the thick of things. I know who is sleeping with whom, and who is mad about it. To paraphrase that famous old saying, "If you find that a nursing home is inevitable, relax and enjoy it."

Here, even the residents who are afflicted with Alzheimer's disease or one of the other dementias are not unhappy, in most cases. They're living completely normal lives in their own little worlds. It's their families who are suffering. Ethel is a good example. Ethel is diminutive, probably less than five feet tall. Her short gray hair is gently waved. She has a perpetual expression of vacant bewilderment. Ethel walks and monologues all day long, but in her mind she has two companions, her long-dead sister and her long-dead father. She uses different voice pitches for each:

I got the one, I got the one that you said. You don't hafta 'cause my fodder was sick. Oh, what are you talkin' about? I don't know, Ethel. I don't know. C'mon, Emily c'mon, c'mon, Emily. My father fell down. My mother is sick I have to get home. My mother's in the hospital. C'mon, c'mon, c'mon, you better come home, Ethel . . . There's nothin there. The son-of-a-bitch. She can't see . . . C'mon, c'mon, Emily. Don't you want to have Ethel and me together? Sure I do. I love it. I love it. *No, Emily, I live right here. I live right here* (singsong). And I go there every day. I see my mother. She went home and she wanted to see little Emily. *Get em on, get em on, get em on, we're gonna eat, we're gonna eat. We're gonna have a few right here* (singsong). I can't find it. I looked all over . . . *I love you, oh, I love you* (singsong). You oughta see the way Ethel got there last night. Why because you got hit, got hit over there . . . C'mon Nick, c'mon, are ya comin? Yes, all right I'll be there in five minutes. Five minutes. . . . Get em on, get em on, get em on. Ya God damn fool, ya God damn fool . . . they were very pretty. She had ten and I had ten

and we both stood there and we looked at each other and
she said to me you look like a monkey and I said well if I
look like a monkey then you must look like a, I don't know
what . . .

Most of the time I think Ethel's cute, but not when she
gets too close. The other day I was seated at the luncheon table.
Ethel was standing beside me and doing her monologue in my
left ear.

I said, "Ethel, shut up, you're driving me crazy."

She looked at me, and in her slow, gentle monotone she
said, "Aw, you were crazy before you came here."

The aides and nurses gained a new respect for Ethel.
When their raucous laughter died down, they expressed their
astonishment that she, too, was aware of what they had known
all along.

The "normal life" the dementia residents have here
includes worrying too. Worrying is the same for these people
as it is for people with a fully functioning brain. The
conversation one day between an aide and Eddie, eighty-eight
years old, went like this:

The aide went into Eddie's room to get him up from his
nap.

Eddie: "I'm worried about my mother."

Aide: "What's the matter?"

Eddie: "She's sick. It's her blood."

Aide: "I wouldn't worry. They can help all kinds of
        blood problems today. How old is she?"

Eddie: "Thirty-nine."

Aide: "She's young and vigorous. Nothing to worry
        about."

Eddie: "Another thing."

Aide: "What?"

Eddie: "I have trouble getting through that gang down at
the corner to get my ticket for the streetcar."

And while this sort of thing is going on in the wings, alert
and oriented residents are playing trivia, or doing a crossword
puzzle, or may be playing basketball in the adjacent activities
room. For our part, Mildred, Thelma, Rudy (my ex-husband),
and I are playing pinochle in the dining room.

Rudy is tall. He measured five eleven when he was a
soldier. He is of Czechoslovakian descent, balding, and thin
with a lean face and an aquiline nose. He is eighty-one years
old and has the energy of a healthy seventy-year-old. His
irascibility is tempered by his good-heartedness. Three years
after I entered Elderwood, Rudy's and my beloved daughter
Susan died from cancer at the age of thirty-three. Our mutual
grief over her death reestablished our relationship, and Rudy
has been a daily visitor for the past ten years.

Thelma was a cheerleader who married her high school
sweetheart, the football hero. At the age of eighty-six, her
delicate features attest to the beauty she must have been.

And Mildred is amazing. At the age of seventy-five her
brown hair is only lightly flecked with gray. She still has a
proclivity for numbers. When someone asks the bingo caller if
a certain number was called, Mildred will answer "yes" or "no"
immediately, even though she might not have that number on
her own cards. And she's always right.

Who needs a working left arm when she's got that many
marbles?

December 6

I know Susan's death is a subject I must talk about, but I
dread it. I was never able to assuage my grief. In a facility of
this type there is no privacy for the kind of grief I needed to

expend. If I cried everybody came running. "What are you crying about?" It's an if-you're-crying-you-must-be-comforted mentality. I didn't have the luxury of sobbing. I still can't go to the cemetery without crying.

When Susan was twenty-six years old she moved from our house into a third floor walk-up apartment across from the University of Buffalo, where she was a secretary at the School of Social Work. Over the next several years, she endured two broken love affairs. In February of '83, when she was thirty-one, she got a Shih-Tzu puppy. I suspect she was still hurting. Every night after work, she took the puppy to Rudy's house so it could run in his fenced-in yard (I had moved out the previous August). Rudy suggested she might as well move back in. She loved her apartment, but Rudy said he'd like the company, and she'd have the advantage of lower expenses. So in August of '83, she moved back into Rudy's house.

The following year she noticed that she had enlarged lymph nodes, but she ignored them. Eventually she had bouts of fatigue for no apparent reason. When these became more than she could cope with, she went to the doctor, who predicted Hodgkin's disease.

I will never forget the sensation I felt when Rudy came over to tell me, "They think Susan has Hodgkin's disease." A knife went through my gut—instantly. It was palpable, not just a figure of speech. Little did I know then that it would have been better if it had been Hodgkin's, which is treatable. Further tests proved she had *non*-Hodgkin's lymphoma. Non-Hodgkin's lymphoma is resistant to treatment. She was in the fourth stage.

She went through the chemotherapy routine anyway. It looked for a while as if the cancer was breaking up, but then something was said about a mutation and the treatments being hopeless. I was able to visit her several times a week by hiring a van, but I wasn't able to do anything like cooking her healthful meals. I have an idea, probably erroneous, that some good nutrition may have helped. (She did, in fact, get some good nutrition from Kathy, who brought things to her frequently.)

On the morning of January 11, 1985, Rudy called me and said I'd better come to the hospital. I dressed as fast as I could while a nurse called a van. By the time I got to Susan's room she could no longer talk, but she mouthed the words, "I love you." Then she closed her eyes and gradually slept away. She died on January 11, 1985, in our cancer research hospital. She was only thirty-three.

Susan was a smoker (as were Rudy and I), but the primary cancer was not lung cancer, so I don't think smoking was a contributing factor. I think job stress was. Our former governor had put a freeze on state job hiring. Susan had been working in a department that was extremely short staffed for some years. She was a perfectionist, which contributed to her stress.

One day when Susan was about twelve years old, she walked to the Boulevard Mall through the fields, which were plentiful around our house at that time. She wasn't back when I thought she should be back, so I began to worry. More time went by, and I worried more. She finally showed up, happy with her small purchases. My worry turned to relief, and then to anger. I berated her unjustly.

I sometimes think this is what will happen when I get to heaven. I'll find her happy as a lark and bawl her out good for having caused me all this grief.

2

Traditions

December 11, 1995

THE SANTA CLAUS SEASON is upon us once again, my fourteenth here. There are two things I dread: poinsettias and "The Twelve Days of Christmas." I hate them both. Somebody asked how I could hate the partridge in the pear tree—it's a Christmas tradition. The people who made it tradition certainly have more tolerance for repetition than I have.

December 14

I wheeled around pedaling my wares this morning. A few of our residents' family members make things for us to raffle at Christmas time, Valentine's Day, and Easter by knitting, crocheting, or other talented means. This time we had an afghan and several wreaths, made by different processes and all beautiful. The money goes into our residents' council fund. I am the bookie and the raffle ticket seller. I fell into the job years ago for reasons that have been obscured by time, but I presume it was because I was the only person with both the motivation and the capability. Anything that is to be raffled is displayed on top of the piano in the activities room. However, not every visitor goes back there, and the staff doesn't always notice things sitting there, so I have to sell aggressively.

On the two weekends before Christmas I sit in the lobby with the prizes displayed on a table so the visitors will have a chance to participate in the raffle. Sometimes I wheel around with some of the items displayed on my lap and sell tickets to the staff by threatening job termination if they don't buy. I beg if they're not the easily intimidated type. On this particular day an aide promised to buy later. She said her money was downstairs in her locker. After lunch I approached her again.

"Not right now," she said.

"Listen, I know a hit man," I threatened. "He owes me a couple of favors and he's a specialist in breaking kneecaps."

She turned to her coworker and said, "I have to go down to my locker and get some money. Jean's threatening me."

You have to be creative in the sales business.

December 22

I just got back from lunch at Angelo's Italian Manor. There are a group of us who have lunch once a month. The group was Rosalia's idea. Rosalia is a beautiful Italian girl in her mid-thirties with a hairstyle like the mother in Family Circus (only Rosalia got hers first). She used to be an activities aide here. Eight years ago she left to have a baby, and our association ended. She came back three years ago, and when she left again last March to have another baby, she suggested meeting once a month because she didn't want to lose contact this time.

This month's lunch group included Rosalia, Faith and Harry (the daughter and son-in-law of a resident), Bernadette and Whitney (weekend receptionists), my ex-husband Rudy, and me. My roommate Joan and her friend Amelia couldn't join us for dinner this time. (When my savings ran out, Medicaid changed my room status. I have now had three roommates for many years, Joan being the most mobile of the current three.)

Joan is a petite seventy-one year old with short, curly red hair and soulful brown eyes. She has Parkinson's disease, which causes her head to bend way over to the right and makes it difficult for her to project her voice. She has arthritis, and she had a botched knee replacement, both of which cause her great pain. The leg with the bad knee was amputated, but the phantom pain keeps her pain level high. Still, she has a valiant spirit that enables her to keep on enjoying some of life's goodies—most of the programs in the activities department (especially bingo), TV, outings, and just plain camaraderie. Everyone adores her.

Amelia is her dear friend with whom she used to work at the telephone company. She is in her mid-fifties, tall, blonde, very slim, and has a pretty face and one of the two most delightful laughs I've ever heard. She says she used to be fat, but it's hard to believe. Amelia is a daily visitor and a volunteer. She looks after Joan's needs and the needs of others.

Trixie, who works in laundry, couldn't make it to lunch either.

We eat in a restaurant if the weather permits and order take-outs in the activities room during the winter months in deference to Joan and me, who are in wheelchairs. Even though this is a winter month, we went out anyway in celebration of the season. Rosalia went in the wheelchair van with me because Rudy went to pick up Peggy, our youngest daughter, from the airport. She flew in from Dallas at just the right time to eat with us.

Angelo's was like fairyland. All the Christmas trees that decorated the room had snow on them and white lights. They were growing in a blanket of snow beside houses half buried in snow. The room we ate in had a royal blue ceiling peppered with white lights to simulate stars. It was glorious. A lot of people think Angelo's is gaudy, and it is, but it's fun gaudy. It's also very popular. I had filet mignon for the first time in years. I could have made a meal out of their appetizers—chopped tomato, onion, basil, and parsley that had been marinated in olive oil until thick. It was then spread on French bread and warmed in the oven. Good conversation always enhances a meal, so the whole shebang was exhilarating. We vowed to do the same thing next year.

December 23

I got a Christmas card from Val today, and it saddened me. Sam is dead. Val was my aide when I was home. She was a tiny little thing, cute as a button, and only about six years younger than me. She came every Thursday and bed-bathed me and did some dusting and vacuuming, and then we played Scrabble—even running into her own time. Sam was another of her charges. He lived in an apartment house a couple of miles down the road. He had cancer, diabetes, polyps, and I don't know what all. She saw him daily, and he lived for Val and their Scrabble games. It was drop-dead competitive.

Val never lost her sense of adventure. One July day, while in her mid-fifties, she said to Sam, "How would you like to go on a cruise?" Sam, despite his physical liabilities, apparently never lost his sense of adventure either. They each paid one thousand dollars immediately for an October Caribbean cruise. This had to be done furtively because the aides were not allowed to take their charges out. Liability, I suppose.

When the day for departure came, Val was on penicillin for strep throat, but having paid a grand, she was determined to go ahead with their plans. Sam told the agency that contracted

Val that he was going to visit his sister in Miami—which was true. He does have a sister in Miami, and she met them for lunch. When the agency called to ask Val to take another client during Sam's absence, her husband told them Val was on penicillin because of a strep throat—which of course was true too.

The trip was just short of disaster. They found the doorway to their stateroom was too narrow to admit a wheelchair. There were no other empty staterooms. Val and the purser (or whoever takes care of these things) went to another ship and measured and found it could accommodate a wheelchair. This ship was going to Puerto Rico, where Val had already been, but at this point there were no options. There was a rather high step to negotiate to get into the stateroom's lavatory. Sam could do it only on his hands and knees. When Sam wanted to smoke a cigar, he had to do it in the passageway because of Val's allergies. Sam wanted to go to the upper deck and gamble in the evening, but Val's infection had depleted her energy by then. The stress fractured their relationship but only temporarily. The bond was strong.

I've had so many people to interact with here at Elderwood. But staying homebound, Sam's only regular connection to the world for so many years was Val. Who could he have told about the frustration of their trip? If it were my vacation, everyone here would have known about it. Twice.

Two years ago Sam had to be transferred to a nursing home because of county budget cuts. This transition was traumatic for both of them. It might have been easier earlier on. Now he's dead. I never met Sam but his life touched mine through Val, and I am saddened.

December 26

Peggy has always been here for the Christmas holidays. Peggy is my youngest and shortest daughter at forty years of age and five feet seven. She is a woman of few words, but her expressive green eyes acknowledge her enjoyment of life. She is a dosimetrist in Dallas, which means she plans the best way to deliver radiation therapy to cancer patients. She has an unfulfilled dream to become a full-time missionary, hopefully in India, so she is also attending evening classes at seminary.

She and Rudy cooked dinner and brought it to the nursing home. Besides turkey they made my favorite: green bean casserole. The standard recipe that everybody has calls for green beans, mushroom soup, and French-fried onions. Rudy added fresh mushrooms, bean sprouts, water chestnuts and soy sauce, which transformed it into a gourmet dish in my opinion.

Elise, a resident, and Maralee, the niece with whose family Elise lived before coming here, ate with us. Elise is ninety-five years old. Parkinson's disease has bent her neck, but it hasn't touched her mind. She still has a beautiful face. Her hair has been a breathtakingly beautiful shade of white since she was a young woman. Her sister was one of my roommates here a few years ago, so our friendship goes back about twelve years.

Maralee is the sexiest looking sixty-year-old I know. She's not vain enough to bother with makeup. She's petite, wears her blonde-highlighted hair in a reverse pageboy, and she has a figure that would allow her to pass for a much younger woman if it weren't for the facial wrinkles. She also has a PhD in English Literature, so I go to her when I have a question about grammar or syntax or any subject at all for that matter.

It was a nice Christmas.

December 28

Mildred, Rudy, and I finished our almost-nightly pinochle session. Rudy wheeled me up to the doorway of my room where I always wait for the aide assigned to my group to put me to bed. But I don't wait in silence.

"Jenny!" I bellowed. "I've been waiting for three quarters of an hour." I say this to the aides frequently. They become indignant because they know I'm lying. But voilà! I have their attention. Jenny was busy with someone else, so she ignored me. I love Jenny.

She's a black woman, somewhere in her forties, with nice features and a nice figure—not more than ten pounds overweight I would guess. She is the only person I know who makes two syllables out of "shit." "Oh, she-it," she'll say when something goes wrong. She's an "upper." She makes you feel good just by entering the room.

Richard, who visits his mother almost every night, came down from the dining room to remark, "I'm going to put this on my calendar. I think this is the first time the three of you have played pinochle without a fight." There was more discussion and laughter about Rudy's short fuse, then Richard left. An aide—not Jenny, she was still ignoring me—pushed me into my room and said accusingly, "Rudy just got out the door and already you're flirting with another man. You whore!" Such language is verboten, of course, but some of the staff and I operate on the theory that what the top brass don't know won't hurt them—or us.

January 3, 1996

THE STATE came this morning for their annual survey. THE STATE is a team of about five people from the New York State Department of Health. Every year they survey each nursing home to make sure the staff is in compliance with the code THE STATE has set. This is probably the main reason nursing home abuse has dropped drastically. What there is, is usually brought to light and punished, at least in New York State. This team questions residents who are "alert and oriented" as we say in the profession.

"How is the food?" is a popular question. "Do they treat you with respect?" Well, not me, they don't. We have a tacit understanding. They call me The Queen, The Pain In The Ass, The Troublemaker, Mean Jean. I tease them unmercifully, and the situation suits us all.

"If you wanted something changed would you be successful in getting it changed?" is another popular question. And the answer is, "If it were feasible, yes." We have a residents' council meeting once a month and we bring up any changes we want at that meeting. The residents' council is composed of whichever residents want to be there. We have a treasury, and we have moneymaking schemes to keep money in it. We have expenses just like any group that is organized under the name of "club." Mostly we raffle things that people make for us. We also sell two-dollar football squares in the fall and five-dollar ones for the super bowl. I am known as the resident bookie. Some people are surprised that we're allowed to do this. The nursing home isn't allowed, but we, as the residents' council, are.

If we want a change that is feasible but hasn't been accomplished, we can keep bringing it up at the residents' council meetings. If it appears in the minutes unresolved for five months, the nursing home will get a citation. It is a far cry from the old days. A citation like this has never happened since I've been here, but it's nice to know we hold a powerful weapon.

Residents often ask to speak to a member of the survey team privately. The chronic complainers have a field day during this time. I think if I were a member of the team listening to some of these complaints, one of my resolutions would be, "Deal with it!" But I guess they can't do that.

The annual survey is a wonderful concept, but I think sometimes they carry it too far. A couple of years ago we were cited because one of our residents was walking down the hall with two or three inches of her slip showing. This was considered undignified. The families of the residents supply the clothes the residents wear, and that's what the staff puts on them. But that fact was not taken into consideration. One year we were cited because one of the cooks picked up a glass of water and took a drink from it while she was stirring something on the stove. According to THE STATE she should have gone to the sink, taken a drink, washed her hands, then returned to the stove. Apparently this rigmarole is standard policy for food inspectors. Sometimes I think the board, which sets policy for these surveys, is made up of twenty-five-year-old MBA graduates who have never been inside a nursing home.

But THE STATE'S emphasis on an adherence to patients' rights is good. They're very strict about preserving the dignity of every resident. The curtains must be drawn around the bed of each one of us, and the door closed, when we're being bathed in bed. They want the aides and nurses to address us by our last names—Mr. or Mrs. So-and-So—unless we give them permission to call us by our first names.

Where I live, they not only call us by our first names, they give us nicknames. Anna is Anna Banana, June is June Bug, I am Jean Bean, George is Georgie Porgie, Betty is Betty Boop, Joe is Jo-Jo, Florence is Flo-Flo, John is John-Boy, Mrs. Cook is Cookie. We wouldn't give up those touches of affection for all the dignity anyone could squeeze out of the State Department.

Our rooms are too small by today's standards, but each year we get a waiver on that issue because we met the standards at the time the nursing home was built thirty-three years ago, and we can't change the size of the rooms. But each year before we get the waiver, the survey team must measure the rooms. They know the size didn't change during the year, but they can't use last year's measurements. It must be done each year. This is your taxpayer's money at work.

When THE STATE comes to measure next year, I may have to belt out "The Twelve Days of Christmas."

3

Champagne Ice

February 18, 1996

ANDREA, AN AIDE, came into our room to get Joan washed and dressed for breakfast. Andrea is a tall, attractive, solid-built, black girl.

"I fixed that SOB," she said.

"What?" I asked.

"I suspected my boyfriend wouldn't get me anything for Valentines Day because he didn't get me anything last year. So, know what I did?"

I didn't have to answer. She could tell by my expression that I wanted to know.

"The day before, I bought myself a big box of expensive candy. When he came over, I offered him some candy from the box 'another man' had given me. That rattled his brains. Know what he did?"

I shook my head. I couldn't wait to hear.

"He went out and bought me a box of Fanny Farmer Dixies, my favorite, and he's hardly left me out of his sight ever since."

I added my two cents worth. "And I'll betcha next year he won't forget, that SOB!"

February 27

When Rudy is in Florida every February, I usually go to bed right after supper and watch *Wheel of Fortune* and *Jeopardy*. Our daughters, Nancy and Kathy, both live in Daytona Beach, so Rudy goes down for about six weeks each winter. Last night I changed my routine. I went into the activities department for a cup of coffee and a little socializing. A tiny woman who wore her grey hair with bangs wheeled over and sat beside me. The conversation went something like this:

"My name is Loretta Boehm—B-o-e-h-m."

"How do you do? I'm Jean."

"My back hurts so. I have osteoporosis. It's uncomfortable to sit.

"Oh."

"What is your name?"

"Jean."

"I'm Loretta. I'm a registered nurse."

"Oh."

"I knew the people who built this place."

"Oh?"

"Did you know them?"

"No" (I-never-had-that-pleasure tone).

"What is your name?"

"Jean."

"What time are you going to bed?"

"About eight o'clock."

"Well, I'll go then too."

"Oh."

"I have osteoporosis. It's uncomfortable to sit."

"Oh" (sympathetic).

"I'm a registered nurse."

"Oh?"

"I know the people who built this place."

"Oh" (How-long-are-we-going-to-keep-this-up tone).

"What time are you going to bed?"

"About eight o'clock."

"Well, I'll go then too."

"Oh" (flat).

"What is your name?"

"Jean."

"I'm Loretta. I'm a registered nurse."

"Oh" (I-give-up tone).

"What time are you going to bed?"

"I think right now might be a good time. Good night."

"Well then, I'll go too."

Every now and then you have to find out whom to avoid in order to keep your sanity.

March 9

Cecile brought in my breakfast tray this morning. Cecile is a pleasingly plump black girl with a beautiful face and a mild temperament. We are fond of each other so we often tease each other. She'll put my breakfast tray down, and with her hands on her hips greet me with, "Look, you're not gonna worry me today."

I will look stern, and in my best gun moll voice say, "Listen, honey, if you want to start something, you've come to the right place." I do this frequently with people I like.

I don't confine myself to traditional breakfast food. Cereal, whether hot or cold, is boring. Bacon and eggs are cholesterol-ridden. My tastes lean toward soup and toasted bagels, salad, or vegetarian chili with fruit for breakfast. Today Cecile brought me a toasted, buttered bagel, a chef salad, and cream of tomato soup.

While I ate, Cindy cleaned out my roommate Nettie's closet and sang a lilting tune:

Hitler was a jerk.

Mussolini bit his weenie,

Now it doesn't work.

No, Cindy is not a dementia resident. She is the head of the housekeeping department—a fun-loving woman who looks like a fifty-five-year-old brunette Barbie doll. She loves to go to Las Vegas and Atlantic City. She is thrilled when she wins, but if she loses, that's okay too.

She's a vigorous and precise housekeeper. Today she was scrubbing Nettie's bed and closet and nightstand. Nettie died a few days ago, at the age of ninety-four, and all the things she used must be scrubbed and sanitized as a routine precaution.

"Did I tell you about the old man whose granddaughter put him in a nursing home?" she asked.

"No," I said, encouraging her.

"He'd lean over to the right, and one of the aides would pass him and push him up straight. He'd lean to the left, and a nurse would pass him and push him up straight. He'd lean forward, and somebody would come along and sit him up straight. His granddaughter came to see him that night. 'How'd it go, Grandpa?' she asked. 'Well, pretty good,' he replied. 'They treat me nice and the food is good. Only one thing—they won't let me fart.'"

Carol stopped in to remark on my hair. She said it looks good now. I had been warned about trying to apply a color rinse on gray hair. A beautician told me it doesn't take as predictably as on other hair shades, but I figured she was just saying that because professionals try to discourage laymen from doing things on their own that deprive the professionals of income. I was wrong. She knew what she was talking about.

But I had wanted to look like Carol. She's a tall, slim, beautiful, former navy nurse with a dynamite personality. I bought Miss Clairol's medium beige blonde. I wanted the beige. I don't like red highlights. So when one of the aides had a chance, she did it for me. While it was taking, Maralee stopped in to say hello. A bit of hair was peeking out from the plastic cap.

"Oh, you're dying your hair red," Maralee said.

Oh, my God, I thought. When the process was over, it had toned down to pink, and I was the butt of many jokes and laughter for a week:

"Why did you dye your hair pink?"

"What color is it, Champagne ice?"

"You look like a hooker."

I've had it shampooed three times since the dye job, and the pink has come out gradually. I like it now. But I still don't look like Carol.

March 10

I was playing pinochle with Thelma, Mildred, and Rudy when the afternoon shift came on. We have a good pinochle group now. We're all "alert and oriented." Dolores, one of the afternoon shift aides, came over and dropped six dollars in my lap.

"I am disgawsted," she said in her Puerto Rican accent.

Sometimes she greets me with, "Hello, Gr-r-r-r-inga," rolling the *r* skillfully. (I try to do the same with, "Hello, Puerto Rican," but I can't do whatever it is you have to do with your tongue and your teeth and the roof of your mouth.) I looked at her quizzically.

"We had three nawmbers and the supplementary, and this is all we got—twelve dollars."

Dolores and I have been going together on the New York State lottery for about five years. Dolores is a beautiful brunette—I mean movie star beautiful—with a beautiful figure, delightful to look at. She has a tale of woe a mile long. For years she bought tickets on the New York State lottery using the same numbers each week. One night her mother-in-law was having pains, so she was rushed to the hospital. Dolores went with her and figured she'd get her lottery ticket on the way home, but her mother-in-law was in such distress Dolores didn't want to leave her. The off-track betting parlor was closed by the time she went home. The next morning she opened the paper, and there were her six numbers—worth six million dollars! That's why I wanted to cast my lot with Dolores. I figured she was lucky. It hasn't worked out that way. We did have four numbers three other times, but the largest pot was $107, or $53.50 each. We keep on, however, week after week. That two dollars buys hope, and we consider that a good bargain.

March 11

Kim was getting my clothes ready to put on me after I got washed. She is a darling little four foot eleven Vietnamese girl with a round face and a button nose. She left Vietnam in June of '88, but didn't get to the United States until August of '89. She was chattering away. I wish I could capture her accent on paper.

"My boyfriend and I didn't know what to do yesterday to have some fun. We didn't want to go to a show. So we went to the casino at Niagara Falls and played blackjack. We lost ninety dollars, and we had fun. That's all we took with us so we couldn't lose anymore."

"You know how to play blackjack?" I asked.

"We didn't, but we do now."

Kim's story is remarkable: Her father was the leader of a plan for a lot of people to escape Vietnam. For a fee, Vietnamese citizens could get the government's permission to build a boat for fishing. The plan was to sail to Malaysia, a three-day trip, in a boat built by her cousin. Their plan was discovered before the final arrangements were finished. Only twenty-three of them, including Kim, managed to get on the boat and get away. Both the navigator and Kim's father were left behind.

The escapees had to circle the islands around Vietnam for a few days because of a storm. This used up gas and food. They had brought a map and a compass, but the fallout from the storm blew both away. They steered at random for thirteen days until the gasoline supply was exhausted. The food and water were gone after three days. Two of the group, a five-year-old girl and a twenty-four-year-old man, died of malnutrition, and their bodies were buried at sea. After nineteen days without food and water, drifting helplessly, a Philippine fishing boat found them and took them to the Philippines. Twenty-two days had passed since they left Vietnam for the three-day trip to Malaysia.

Kim barely knows her father. He was either a prisoner of war or a political prisoner for most of the time she lived in Vietnam. It was only during the occasional times when the family was allowed to visit that she saw him. The more money that crossed palms, the more frequent those times were. Kim's father was arrested and sentenced to fourteen years in jail for his part in the conspiracy. She is attempting to get him an early release and to bring her parents to the States.

It took fourteen months for the papers to be processed in the Philippines so that Kim could come to the United States. While there, she learned a smattering of English. Once she arrived here, she moved in with her godparents, who live in the suburbs. School was terribly difficult at first. Getting to the bathroom was a major operation. She knew the word "bathroom," but her accent was so strong her teacher couldn't understand her. Kim had to draw a picture of two doors with a man on one and a woman on the other. That the teacher could understand.

Contrary to what some might think, Kim does pronounce the letter *L* because it's contained in their alphabet. Interestingly, the Vietnamese alphabet contains twenty-nine letters. There is no *w* or *z,* but there are three *a's,* three *o's,* and two *e's,* each with marks above or below it to indicate the pronunciation.

March 12

One of the aides came into my room chuckling. "Kitty just said to me, 'Somebody told me you were the town drunk, and you're nuts too."

Kitty is probably an Alzheimer's victim. I don't know the diagnoses of our residents, but its obvious that she has one of the dementias. She is one of our most boisterous residents. She is a large woman. She wears glasses, and her straight gray hair goes almost to her shoulders. Most of the time she is calm. Yesterday she and I planned a party and decided whom we'd invite and whom we'd leave out. We considered the Clintons—Hillary is in, but Bill is out.

When she gets loud, it's beyond the definition of the word. All of us think she's funny. That is, we did until the day she hollered, "I gotta go ta the shithouse!" in the middle of the priest's sermon. Now only some of us think she's funny.

March 13

Kim wheeled me down the hall and put me in the shower room. I prefer a shower rather than a bath. The bathtub room is across the hall and down about five feet from the shower room. Just as she was closing the curtain, I caught a glimpse of a black man sitting in a wheelchair outside the tub-room doorway. Knowing we didn't have any black residents currently, I was confused and curious, and I told Kim to open the curtain so I could see who it was. It was Mark, one of the south wing aides, waiting while Jake, one of the residents, luxuriated in his bath.

Jake heard me ask, "Who is that?" He thought I meant him. He translated that into thinking it meant I wanted to see him, and since he was naked, it meant I wanted to see him in the nude.

He said, "Let her look."

His laughter is infectious in most any instance. He has three types of laughter—a chuckle that is a high "hee-hee" type, a loud hearty laugh, and a "hoo-oo" in the manner that boys hoot at girls. He was so delighted by my apparent interest, he went from one type to another to another, interspersed with hoots. It infected Kim and me. Our laughter wasn't exhausted until we reached the idiotic-feeling stage. Jake was still chuckling and hooting at my obvious lust as Mark wheeled him down to his room. It's a nice feeling to know you've made someone's day.

I have a great compassion for Jake. He is only sixty-five years old, tall with rugged good looks and would have been a lady-killer if an auto accident, at the age of twenty-four, had not injured his brain. After months of rehabilitation he was able to handle his job at the Chevrolet plant again. When he was fifty-eight, he suffered a stroke that paralyzed his right side. That's when he came to live at Elderwood. But he is not unhappy. He has bouts of anger—but don't we all—and most of the time he's content and enjoys the activities.

I was sitting in my doorway waiting to be put to bed when the phone in the lobby summoned me.

Rosalia sounded excited. "Did you hear the scoop?"

"What scoop?"

"You didn't hear anything?"

"No." I was puzzled and impatient.

"I'm coming back."

"WHAT?" A low-key shout.

"Wanda [the activities director] called and asked me to work Monday, Tuesday, Wednesday, and Thursday evenings."

We were both excited. Rosalia has a beautiful family—husband, eleven-year-old son, eight-year– and eight-months-old daughters—and a voluptuous figure. She's the only person I've ever known whose boobs stuck out more than her abdomen during pregnancy. Everybody will be excited when they hear she's coming back.

4

Safety in Numbers

(Unless That Large Number Is Your Age)

March 21, 1996

IT'S THE FIRST DAY OF SPRING and everything is white. A good couple of inches of snow fell overnight. The forsythia branches outside my window are loaded with it.

It's also Laura's birthday—her fortieth. Laura is the south wing coordinator (a level above a charge nurse). She's very pretty with a nice figure, and she does not look her age.

She had the day off yesterday and went shopping at the Boulevard Mall. When she came out to go to her car, it wasn't there. *Oh, damn,* she thought. *I forgot where I parked.* She went into the mall again and went out a different door. No luck there either. She went up and down the rows. Through the process of elimination, the horrible truth crept up on her, and there was nothing to do but call the police.

Happy Birthday, Laura.

March 23

I was wearing my red and white dress. I put on my bright red lipstick, trying to match my dress. It made me look as if I were wearing more makeup than usual. Everybody complimented me on how nice I looked. I wheeled down to the dining room, and an activities aide walked over from the activities room.

"Boy, you look nice," he said. "Why don't you look like that every day? We have to look nice every day."

I have a list of people whose butts I'm going to kick if I can ever lift my leg. He was just transferred to Number One.

March 24

Kim was getting me dressed. She mentioned that Bella, a north wing aide, had baked her a birthday cake.

I said, "I know."

"How you know?"

I told her Bella had told me she was going to.

"I want to learn how to do that," said Kim. "I want to bake my own wedding cake."

Kim is twenty-five and determined to remain a virgin until her wedding day. She feels that's the best gift a bride can give her husband.

I said, "If you keep prolonging it, there might not be a wedding. He'll find somebody else."

"So-o-o, then I'll find somebody else."

She's got a good handle on life.

March 25

The police called Laura two days later and said her car had been found wrapped around a tree on Sweet Street. She would have to meet the AAA men there. The cop said, "Don't go alone." Sweet Street is in the heart of the ghetto where drive-by shootings occur—a lot of them.

When she got there, five AAA men were there.

"We never come in this section with fewer than five men," one said.

Laura sat mourning her beautiful Beretta while the men got it on the flatbed truck. Suddenly she heard some pops and the sound of glass breaking.

"Get out of here quick," one of the men yelled. "They're shooting at *us*. We'll meet you back at the police station."

The AAA won't go into that section with fewer than five men, and all that the cop said to Laura was, "Don't go there alone?" What does that mean—bring your mother?

My roommate Joan had her TV on. A reporter was talking about a Rochester man who raped a three-year-old girl. He was caught in the act, so there was no question about his guilt. Kim, who had just brought me my breakfast tray, was of the opinion that they should cut off his penis and let him bleed to death. Liz, who works in physical therapy, thought they should bury him in the desert sand with his hands and feet bound and just his nose and his penis and testicles showing, and let the buzzards have a feast. I'm for anything that would keep him out of the community forever, although I'm not too happy about the community having to pay his room and board.

I think that medical examiners should autopsy the brains of people who commit crimes like that—and the brains of serial rapists, serial murderers, and drive-by shooters—to see if there is a consistent aberration that causes them to do these things—I mean too much testosterone, or lack of a neurotransmitter, or something like that, which could be corrected in time. I know a lot of it is blamed on abusive parents or negligent parents or a childhood of poverty and deprivation, but a lot of people who were raised under those circumstances turn out to be good productive human beings. So how come?

March 27

I woke up at about six o'clock thinking about the movie I had seen the night before—*The Wrong Woman* with Nancy McKeon, whom I love. It was full of tension.

This is one of the great things about living in a nursing home. Most houses are vulnerable—at least in the average person's economic class—but here the building is practically impregnable. I can watch movies that I wouldn't dare watch and read books that I wouldn't dare read at home, reassured by the comforting sights and sounds just outside my door in the hallway.

March 28

On my way to the activities room, I passed one of the residents, Alice, in the hallway.

"It doesn't seem like tomorrow's Christmas, does it?" she asked.

"That's probably because it isn't Christmas."

I think I saved her self-esteem because she said, "Oh, then that's why I didn't get any cards or nothin'."

Our little luncheon group ate behind the iron curtain. That's what I call the folding doors that separate the front half of the activities room from the back half. The front half is always exposed, separated from the dining room by a wide archway. The back half is private when the folding doors are closed. It's furnished with two round, homey-looking tables with tablecloths and chairs, the activity director's desk, a dressing table with mirror, three rockers, an old-fashioned soda fountain chair, a three-tiered-basket table that holds all sorts of stuffed animals, and a complete kitchenette including microwave oven. We use the kitchenette to bake every Tuesday and Thursday mornings, to create our "celebrity chef" luncheon the last Tuesday of every month, and to heat popcorn, pizza, and all kinds of etcetera.

Our luncheon group this month consisted of Faith and Harry, Trixie, Rosalia, Joan, Rudy, and me. Harry brought pizza from his favorite pizzeria. It was delicious. Rosalia had just discovered peach Jell-O and made some for us so we could enjoy her new find. I had asked her to bake a cherry pie according to my made-up recipe. I wanted her to mix a can of Comstock cherry pie filling with a package of frozen cherries and bake it. The pie filling is too thick, and I thought the frozen cherries would thin it out so it would be a little runny. Being a little runny is what lets you know a pie is homemade. She was reluctant, but she did it. It turned out exactly as I pictured it. Marvelous.

March 29

I was eating my breakfast this morning (pizza and two oranges) when Cindy, the head housekeeper, came in. She had just gotten back from Florida. She went with her husband Neal and her brother Larry and his wife Eileen.

One of the highlights was the thirteen-story drop in The Hollywood Tower of Terror building at the MGM studios. It's a sudden drop, and you're not supposed to get in the elevator ride if you have certain health problems such as high blood pressure or heart problems. When Cindy, Eileen, and Neal got in, they discovered Larry wasn't with them. Neal got back out on the pretense of running after Larry, and then neither one of them came back. Cindy and Eileen were embarrassed to show their fear in front of all the kids that were on the ride, but they were about as terrified as if they were on a plane being hijacked.

Bang! In a moment, it was over for everything but their stomachs, which were still on the thirteenth floor. Neal and Larry had gleefully watched on the monitor in the lobby, but since they were the custodians of the money, Cindy and Eileen didn't dare even think of revenge.

As I sat in the dining room, killing time before going to physical therapy, I watched a bowling game in progress in the activities area. They have plastic pins and balls so no one gets hurt. All I could see was Amelia's (Joan's friend and a volunteer) and an activities aide's torsos bobbing up and down. Various "yays" indicated how things were going. The aquarium blocked a clear view, but it was a lovely, warm, cozy feeling looking through the aquarium, through the bobbing torsos, to the late morning sun filtering through the windows on the bowling game.

Rosalia came in at six thirty. It's so good to have her back. It's also good to have her homemade bran muffins back.

April 1

I woke up to a few snow flurries. They stopped soon afterward. I think it was God's April Fools joke.

I had bean soup and grapefruit for breakfast. I could have eaten a whole case of that bean soup.

My friend Penny brought some of the Easter candy orders in during the afternoon. She does beautiful work. She has a chocolate house that's trimmed with a flowered window box and a doorway that she sells for six dollars. It should be at least ten. Her bouquet of chocolate roses in a chocolate basket is gorgeous. The roses are wrapped with foil.

Penny's grandmother died here almost a decade ago. Penny's family—her mother, her father, and her brother—is one of those you feel, after a short acquaintance, that you've

known them all your life. I came here in August of '82, and
Penny's grandmother came in November. The following
February, Penny's father gave me a chocolate penis for
Valentine's Day. I had told the girls (aides) this, so this year
they clamored around Penny asking her if she could make
some for them. Several of them ordered suckers, but Barbara, a
north wing aide, wanted the large one—balls and all—for a
centerpiece.

April 2

I finished reading *Snake and The Spider* four days ago. I
can't get it out of my mind. It's a true story about two boys
from a small town in Michigan who drive to Daytona Beach
for a vacation. They were seventeen and nineteen. In their
naiveté they fall in with the wrong men and are brutally killed
for their car. The appeal of the story is how the private
investigator tracked down the killers. It took four months, and
the author described the parents' agony so poignantly that there
were times I cried.

This happened in 1978. The lives of two large happy
families were ruined. The frightening part is that the book said
the perpetrators would probably be released this year. I guess
because the Florida jails are so crowded.

Did I mention how much I like our impregnable building
here?

April 4

When our afternoon pinochle game broke up, Rudy
couldn't find his cap. After looking all around he said, "I bet
Josie took it."

Right after he left, a north wing aide came in with it. "Josie had it in her pants," she said, "and her pants were wet and dirty. I washed it as best I could, but it still smells."

"Don't tell him," I said.

"Gosh, don't tell him," she echoed.

"Oh my God, no," was all you heard amid the laughter.

But when he came back in the evening, I did tell him.

His reaction was predictable. "Oh, shit!" But it was mild because he's very fond of Josie. "I'll put it in the washer and see what happens."

April 6

Dick, who comes to see his mother almost every night, stopped by our table while Mildred, Rudy, and I were playing cards, with his most recent *bon mot*. "What did Adam say to Eve in the Garden?"

I shrugged and shook my head slightly.

"You'd better stand back. I don't know what this thing is going to do."

He has one for us every evening. Mostly they're corny—"I cut my finger but it didn't bleed for three days. Oh—I have tired blood." Sometimes they're clever. When I was selling raffle tickets and football squares at the same time, his opening remark to me one evening was, "Since I met you, I've had to take out a mortgage on my house." Sometimes they're risqué like the Adam and Eve one, but they always add to the general good humor of the evening.

April 10

Easter was the seventh, and I was in bed for most of Friday, Saturday, Sunday, and Monday. I had an unsettled stomach and a fever that made me want to sleep. It's delightful to have no pressing responsibilities and to be able to sleep when you feel that way.

April 12

Margaret, the dietary supervisor, and I were chatting while I was sitting at my table after lunch.

"I heard they put your roommate on a feeding tube," she said.

"What!" I was horrified.

Lyd, one of my three roommates, has been in the hospital for several days. She has been unable to speak or move ever since I've known her. Her body has to be turned at regular intervals to prevent bedsores. I don't know if she had a stroke or what. She often responds with her eyes or a smile, and it always warms the heart of whoever evoked the response.

Her dear friend and companion, who died a couple of years ago, told me that Lyd had two sons and buried them both—one when he was seven or eight and the other when he was fifty-six. The friend didn't know the circumstances. I often wonder if these tragedies contributed to her journey here.

I love Lyd, and I don't want to lose her as a roommate, but she is almost ninety-eight years old. She has no family to make decisions for her. A feeding tube through her nose! She has suffered enough lying day after day in a body that won't allow her to make satisfying contact with another human being. New York State law says, however, that if you haven't made your specific desires known in writing regarding life support measures, then the state must do whatever it can to prolong your life. I don't know how it's worded, but that's the idea.

Well, as Ann Landers says, "Don't forget, 50 percent of all doctors graduated in the bottom half of their class." I think this applies to lawmakers too.

Lyd, I think you hit the jackpot with the policy makers and the policy enforcers who are right down there among the bottom half. The only thing worse than having your car stolen on your birthday is having strangers insist you keep on having birthdays no matter the cost.

5

A Talent for Quality

April 12, 1996

EVERYBODY'S COMPLAINING. So far April's been like winter.
It's okay by me. I hate the sun. But I am worried about the
strawberry and cherry crops. Rudy always picks both and
freezes some, and I do enjoy them.

(Shortly after I wrote this, I read in the paper that this
weather is good for the fruit crop. Sometimes it warms up early
and the trees bud, then a spring frost kills them. That doesn't
happen in weather like this.)

Trixie, who works in laundry, is back from Florida, and
she brought me some Vidalia onions. I love Vidalia onion
sandwiches on toast. Pile on the onions and add some
mustard—gourmet eating. For those of you who don't know
about Vidalia onions—they're onions grown in a certain area
of Georgia. They're sweet as apples, and you can eat them like
one. No one knows why they are so different. The soil has been
analyzed, and scientists can find no reason for it. But the
onions don't know that, so they go right on doing their thing.

Speaking of Trixie, she is one of the most fantastic single
mothers I know. She used to be an activities aide but moved to
laundry once all her kids were in school. (She can fit in more
hours that way.) She has been divorced for eight years. She is
petite and her curly hair grows out rather than down, so her

beautiful little face is framed by a dark blonde halo. I
frequently tell her it's time to get it cut. Her mother lives in
West Virginia, so I feel I have to take over some of the
motherly duties.

Trixie has two girls, twenty and ten years of age, and two
boys, fifteen and thirteen. Deanna, the eldest and as pretty as
Trixie, is out on her own. Trixie brought her through
adolescence with their relationship intact. Trixie's youngest is
going to be prettier than her mom and is heading toward a
valedictorian-of-her-class role. Between transporting kids to
and from dancing lessons, violin lessons, cheerleading practice,
basketball, and hockey practice, Trixie has very little time for
herself. But, as her father pointed out to her during a telephone
conversation in which Trixie was wallowing in self-pity,
"Don't ever forget—active parenting may be work, but it's
better than sitting in the juvie holding center waiting for a kid
that'll never amount to nothin'."

April 13

Terry called to tell me that Robin, her granddaughter, is
back in the hospital. Terry is my oldest friend—I mean this
both ways—with whom I still have frequent contact. We were
neighbors when we lived on Kenilworth Avenue. Her daughter
Jessica and my daughter Nancy are the same age, almost
fifty-two years old. Jessica is the sole parental caregiver (she
divorced in March of '92) of a twenty-two-year-old daughter
who has multiple sclerosis. I'm fond of Jessica, and it hurts me
to realize that now the focus of her life is coming home from
work to take care of Robin.

At the time of Robin's diagnosis two years ago, I felt that
if you were destined to get MS, this was a good time.
Betaseron, which had been developed by then, was highly

touted as the newest help for MS. Robin was put on it in March of '95, but it hasn't helped her yet. Her doctor said that it sometimes takes a year or two to take hold. Prednisone has helped, but only temporarily. She's good for three days, then back to square one. She has lost a lot of weight and is in bed most of the time. It has been my observation that the younger you get MS, the faster it progresses. But that's only an observation. I've had no professional confirmation.

Robin is adopted, and she has expressed a desire to know who her birth mother is before she dies. Jessica wrote to Oprah Winfrey last month and asked if she could help with this monumental task, but so far no response.

Not everyone had bad news to complain about or commiserate over today. Some took their bad news in stride.

Rosalia came in to work at six thirty as usual. She looked at the activities calendar for April and said, "Do you know anything about this talent show on the twenty-third?"

"Yeah, we scheduled it at the Quality of Life meeting."

"What's it about?"

"Different people are going to do different acts."

"Like what?"

"Well, Harry's going to cut Mr. C.'s hair while sing—"

"Harry?" she interrupted. "Harry can sing?"

"Oh, he's terrific."

"So he'll be the singing barber?" Her gales of laughter cut me short. "Okay, what else?"

"Helen is going to do the Charleston if we can find the right music."

"Helen in laundry? She can do the Charleston?"

"You should see her. And I'm going to read a story or a fable or something."

Now her laughter almost choked her. "So whose idea was that?"

"Wanda's"

"Where are you going to get the fable?"

"From Wanda."

"So where's the talent? You can read?" Her affectionate sarcasm accelerated our laughter.

"Oh, God, I have to see this, but I can't. I'll be picking the kids up from school. Oh, my God, what'll I do? I don't want to miss this."

April 20

It's still cold and wintry. I went to my computer after I got dressed and, as has been happening lately, I bent my head to take a little nap and slept until lunchtime. When I complained about my drowsiness to my roommate's daughter, she suggested it might be due to medication I'm on. I am taking Tegretol, an anti-seizure medication for trigeminal neuralgia, of which I had my first attack in March of last year. Carol, the nurse with the good hair, looked up the possible side effects at lunchtime, and sure enough drowsiness and fatigue were two of them. I'm trying to forget the others. They were worse. As Carol said, "Drowsiness is better than pain." And such pain as that caused by trigeminal neuralgia I've never known. I've heard it said, and I've seen it in print that it's known as the most excruciating pain known to humanity, and I can well believe it.

April 22

The forsythia outside my window is in bloom, and I can't get enough of looking at it. Forsythia is not one of my favorite flowers, but this is a special circumstance. I've been here almost fourteen years, and this is the first year I've seen it. It's always been outside my window, but they always cut it back in the fall, making it too low to see from inside the building. Last year Al, the head of maintenance, wouldn't let them cut it back, and I can't express what joy I'm getting out of it. My room has three adjacent windows so it's a wide expanse of forsythia. Thanks, Al. I owe you one.

April 23

We had the talent show today. It wasn't too bad. A lot of people who were supposed to be in it didn't show for one reason or another. Dr. Wayland furnished the piano accompaniment for Helen's rendition of the Charleston. She has such grace for a woman her age and build. By build I don't mean heavy, but she's solid and not too far from retirement age. Anyway, it was a good opening act, and she said she did it because I asked her to. She wouldn't have done it otherwise.

I couldn't read a fable from the book Wanda gave me because I couldn't hold it open with one hand, and I had to hold the microphone with my right hand. So I read a page from *The Bare Facts*, the nursing home newspaper I used to write. "Sigmund Wollman's Reality Test" from Robert Fulghum's book *Uh-Oh* is one of my favorite philosophical discourses. It's about separating the big problems from the little ones and ends with these great words: "Life *is* inconvenient. . . . Life is lumpy. And a lump in the oatmeal, a lump in the throat, and a lump in a breast are not the same lump. One should learn the difference."[1]

People were so rude. The ones in the back huddled in a group and talked among themselves. The volunteers, passing cookies and drinks to those in the audience, walked back and forth in front of me. Those who were seated in the dining room were able to concentrate, apparently, because Loretta asked me for a copy of what I read.

Rosalia did make it—after she picked the kids up—and it was a good thing. Her nine-year-old Christine, who is cute as a button, did an unscheduled number and that helped to make up for the no-shows. She was a big hit.

April 24

Dick's mother died this morning. She was a sweet, uncomplaining woman—and we'll miss her—but the loss of her son's nightly visits will be a bigger blow. He is such fun with his constant jokes or puns, and he contributes so much just by being here. You get to be very fond of (and very dependent on) social interaction with some members of other people's families. When their visits are cut off because of the death of their relative, it's such a depressing time for those of us who were close.

April 25

If anyone has reason to complain this month, it's Jackie, one of the nurses. She came to work this morning because she felt she would be better off keeping busy, but the supervisor sent her home. Before she left, she told us the story: her thirty-two-year-old sister was murdered the night before. The sister's boyfriend was trying to extract money so he could buy more drugs. The more Jackie's sister refused, the madder he got. Finally he pulled out a knife and stabbed her in the chest. Then he dragged her out onto the sidewalk, sat on her chest, and choked her. All of this took place in front of the woman's two children, a nine-year-old boy and an eight-year-old girl.

The boyfriend broke the handle off the knife blade and threw the handle in the backyard. He threw the blade onto the roof of a grocery store behind the house. Then he called the police protesting, "I didn't do it, I didn't do it." That sounds pretty much like a confession to me. I guess the police thought so too. He was hauled off to jail.

Talk about a depressing time.

April 26

I had my first ear of corn on the cob for the season. It looked tough but it was delicious. It must have been several days old because it had to be hauled up from Florida, and who knows how long it was in the supermarket, and I had it for a whole day before we cooked it, but it was sweet. I don't know why our farmers can't grow the same kind of corn as the Florida farmers. Our corn loses sugar fast, and some of it doesn't have much to begin with.

April 28

Rosalia came in at her regular time. She has been complaining about her seven-month-old daughter, crying so much. It's been going on for days, and Rosalia's upset and tired from lack of sleep. Debbie, an aide, asked if the baby was on an antibiotic. Rosalia said yes and told her what it was. Debbie told her to change to a lactose-free formula.

Debbie has been an aide here for thirteen years. She was twenty-one years old when she started. She had no idea what the work was about. It includes cleaning up incontinent residents and changing diapers—big time. At the time she started, it also included a supervisor who would have made a marine sergeant look like Uncle Remus. At the end of her first day she went home in tears.

"Ma!" she sobbed. "All I've been doing all day is cleaning up crotches and being told how to do it by Attila the Hun."

It's a wonder she came back.

April 28

Rosalia just discovered hummus, and she brought me a sample. She's crazy about it. Try it. You'll like it if you can get past the color. It looks like baby-do. I use it as a spread on toasted bagels. It's mashed chickpeas with different things added—like garlic and other herbs and spices. It's better for you than butter.

April 29

Rosalia came in with a smile of gratitude on her face and a hug for Debbie. She changed formulas, and now the baby is sleeping beautifully. I once read that more psychotherapy goes on at ten in the morning over the kitchen table than in any psychiatrist's office. Is this true for general medicine as well?

May 1

Today is Rudy's eighty-second birthday. I treated him to lunch at the Chinese restaurant that's within wheelchair-pushing distance. The wind was fierce and cold. We had to hide behind buildings at regular intervals for relief. Rosalia baked him an apple pie, and we ate it after I got in bed. She even brought candles and matches. She couldn't participate because she had to call bingo. Our bingo players are addicts. A five-minute delay would have thrown the room into pandemonium.

May 3

Mr. C., our administrator, was reading excerpts from *Old Possum's Book of Practical Cats* by T. S. Eliot to a small group of residents. After about fifteen minutes he said, "If you don't want me to read any more, just tell me."

Lottie hollered, "No more, no more." Since she was the only dissenter, and in all likelihood didn't know what she was dissenting about, Mr. C. moved her over five feet and resumed reading.

Lottie is a gentle, tiny woman with dainty features. She must have been a beauty in her day. She still would be if she'd allow them to cut her long, straight white hair. She often chants, "God is great, God is good. Let us tank Him for our food," emphasizing each word and elongating *great* and *good* and *food*. She leaves out the *h* in *th* words, as people with a Polish accent usually do.

One day she was sitting in the north wing hallway lamenting the temporary loss of her dentures. "Where's my teet? Did anybody see my teet? God is g-r-e a-t. God is g-o-o-d. Who da hell's got my teet?"

May 7

Terry called. Yesterday, Jessica's friend helped her put the information about Robin's adoption on the Internet, hoping someone would recognize the name and birth date. She was born January 13, 1974, and christened Stephanie Jane. They have other information about the mother and father that they entered. They're hoping it's enough to jar someone's memory or someone's conscience.

May 8

Liz, a physical therapy aide, came into my room after breakfast to give me exercises in hopes of increasing my range of motion. I asked her why her hair looked so awful. She said, "My car was parked under a tree, and while I was cleaning my windshield, a bird shit on my head. I had to wash it after I got here."

There's a benefit to living mostly indoors.

May 9

My daughter Kathy, my grandson Curt, and Curt's girlfriend were visiting from Daytona Beach. Curt is my eldest grandson. He looks like a twenty-six-year old cross between Jack Kemp and Michael J. Fox. Even though it was raining, we went through with our plans to eat at the Chinese restaurant. Kathy and Curt's girlfriend drove. I was going to have my hair done the next day, so there was no need for an umbrella. (So much for living mostly indoors.) With Curt pushing me, and Rudy bringing up the rear, we caravanned up Walnut Avenue.

We were waiting for the light to change at Mulberry Drive when a woman stopped her car, thrust an umbrella out the window, and called to Rudy, "Here, take this." The traffic was heavy, and there was no time to protest. When Rudy opened it, we found Liz Claiborne's signature on one of the panels. It happened so fast that I didn't see who was driving the car, so now I don't know whether I'm the proud owner of a Liz Claiborne umbrella or whether some acquaintance will stop in one day and say, "May I have my umbrella back?"

May 10

Today is the last day of employment for our beloved Director of Nursing, Pat LaPorta. Her family is moving to Arizona. She has already found employment there, but perhaps they will find the summers too hot and move back here. Is it possible? Pat is so easy to talk to—sympathetic, understanding, a good listener. She has been loved and respected by both the staff and the residents. Good luck to you, Pat!

May 12

It was three o'clock in the morning. I rang my call light to be taken off the bedpan. Ronnie answered my call. Ronnie is a handsome black man, and most of the girls go gaga over him.

The procedure is—after he takes me off the bedpan and makes fun of my big fanny—I bend one knee, he bends the other, and I push myself up in the bed toward the headboard to reposition myself. This time Ronnie left his arm under my knees after he bent the left one. He had his other hand on top of my knees in a protective manner, and I said, "Take your arm away." It felt like restraints to me, and I felt it impeded my intent, so I said again, "Take your hand away."

"Just like a woman," he snarled. "Complaining all the time, no matter what we do." He pitched his voice higher. "Don't do this, do that. No, you're not doing it right." He returned his voice back to normal. "Nothing we ever do is right. There's just no pleasing you." Then, as he stalked out of the room, he added, "Stop being a female and go to sleep."

I accepted the good-natured teasing for what it was and turned over with a grin on my face.

6

Hairbrushes Make Your Hair Frizzy

May 13, 1996

VALUABLE THINGS I HAVE LEARNED since I came here:

1. I had never heard the word *dildo* until I came here. I guess I never read those kinds of books. Erle Stanley Gardner was more my speed. In fact, I blame him partly for my hemorrhoids. I would go into the bathroom with a Perry Mason mystery. When I was through with what I had gone in for, I couldn't get up because I was in the middle of a chapter. So I promised myself I'd get up at the end of the chapter, but I couldn't because there was too much tension hanging, so I had to read on. When my legs and feet were numb, I had no choice, and over the years the damage was done.

2. Hairbrushes make your hair frizzy. Mildred told me this, and everybody agreed. Boy, talk about feeling dumb.

3. I thought it was just folklore that people become more agitated and rambunctious during a full moon. Here it's really noticeable. Last night was a good example. One of the nurses answered my call light and said the place was really crazy. Estelle and Carrie were two of the residents who were the most restless. The nurse said Estelle couldn't sleep, so at three in the morning Carrie

began pushing her down the hallway in her wheelchair. Estelle, trying to hit Carrie with her shoe, was hollering, "Stop it! Stop it!" while Vivian, one of the aides, chased them.

4.   It's easier to drink warm water if you're not thirsty than it is to drink cold water. I had to drink eight ounces of water with fiber pills I was taking. I like ice water and tried to drink my eight ounces that way. Couldn't do it. Heated the water, and there was no problem. I could have gone on indefinitely.

5.   Certain bingo cards win more often than others. I don't play often, but when I do I take card number sixty-one as one of my cards, and it wins every time. My other card, chosen at random, hardly ever wins. Mildred has found this to be true too. She picks cards that have certain numbers and that eliminate certain numbers, and she wins from two to six times every session. I think between the two of us we have elevated this theory to the level of scientific fact.

6.   The most complete protein is found in eggs. I was surprised. I always thought it was meat.

7.   Hydrogen peroxide takes out bloodstains. How valuable that would have been during my active life!—and I never found it out until I was three quarters of a century old.

8.   Ground bamboo is undetectable in an autopsy. That's one of the first things I heard after I came here. I don't know if this is true, and I don't know of what use it would ever be to me, but the insinuation is intriguing. I tucked it away in a corner of my memory just in case.

9.   Cut lilacs are notorious for lasting only a few days. To prolong their life, pick them early in the morning, and pick them before the buds open completely.

10.   Sleeping on silk pillowcases will keep your hair from falling out. Sleeping on cotton pillowcases is what has caused that bald spot in the back of my head. I'll be darned!

May 15

I'm seventy-six years old today. I've been in the "elderly" class for a few years now and I'm scared. The thought of being elderly is abhorrent. I'm afraid this will be documented in a newspaper article some day. You often see in the paper an article headed something like, "Elderly Woman Robbed of Life Savings. Elvira Winkerstein, age seventy-three, let three men, claiming to be from the electric company, into her home . . ." or "Elderly Man Hit by Car while Crossing Main Street. Elmer Kadiddlehopper, age seventy-one, was injured severely when he was struck . . ."

This is frightening. Here I am seventy-six years old on the outside, but I feel twenty-two on the inside. And If I were involved in an accident the headline would read, "Elderly Woman Hurt while . . ." Ohmigawd!

May 20

Darla, who works in the dietary department, had said she wanted to take me out for a birthday dinner. So five days after the fact, she and her friend Sally took me to the very popular Greek restaurant just one block away, easily pushable. After we had dinner (they have the best chicken *souvlaki* and rice pudding) we talked a while over coffee and the small birthday cake Darla had ordered. Then they pushed me over to a nearby plaza, and we browsed through the stores. Darla got tired of carrying the leftover cake. She set the box down in the landscaping around one of the department stores. It was still there on our way back. I wanted to pick it up, but Darla and

Sally wouldn't let me. They were afraid of ants. I said we could pick off the ants if there were any. They were adamant and didn't try to hide their disgust at my standards of hygiene.

I wanted some lilacs, my favorite flower. We have light purple bushes in our backyard, but I wanted some dark purple to mix with them. It was dark by now, so they wheeled me up and down side streets, peeking in backyards for a lilac bush so we could steal some. No luck. So we went on the other side of Walnut Avenue and wheeled down Bernard Drive. We came across a group of kids. I asked them if they knew of any lilac bushes in the area. They pointed to a house down the street. I asked if they knew if the people were home.

One kid said, "She's dead."

This was just what we were looking for—a dead woman with a lilac bush. We could see it from where we were. It was even out in front. The lilacs were white, but that was just as good. They'd look nice mixed with the light purple. What incredible luck! Sally had brought her nail clippers, so she clipped me a big bouquet.

We started up the driveway to see if there were any flowers in the backyard we could steal, but when we saw a light in the kitchen window we backed off. Whispers and giggles carry easily in the night air, and you can't make a fast getaway in a wheelchair.

We hurried back home so we could get the lilacs in water. It was ten thirty by then. The nurse on duty was mad because I had forgotten to tell her I was going out. What did I care? I had my lilacs.

May 21

We have some female residents who curse and swear. The daughters of many of these residents say, "My mother never talked like that when she was herself. My friends don't believe me when I tell them how she swears." Lucille is one of these. She sits in her doorway saying, "Ya no good f _ _ _ _ _ _ son-of a-bitch, ya goddam bastard" to no one in particular for an hour or more at a time.

Norbert is a male resident, thoroughly confused, but occasionally he utters coherent phrases or sentences, sometimes belligerently. "I'm going to have this place closed down. I'm going to have you girls put in jail."

On this particular day I was wheeling up to my room when I heard a lot of laughter at the nurses' station. Not wanting to miss anything I went to see the cause of the merriment. They told me what had just happened:

Norbert wheeled over to Lucille and told her how much he still loved her, that she was as beautiful as ever.

She replied her usual, "Ya f_____ son-of-a bitch."

Tears came to his eyes. "After fifty years, don't you know me anymore?"

"Leave me alone or I'll tear your cock off, that is if ya have one, ya goddam f_____ son-of-a-bitch."

The nurse pulled him away and turned him around. "Norbert," she explained, "that isn't your wife Millie. You two don't even know each other."

Norbert brightened. "Oh!"

He turned his chair around, wheeled back to Lucille's doorway, and told her, "I have good news for you. We don't even know each other."

May 22

Ernie brought some lilacs in today for the activities room. His wife died here a few years ago, and he still brings us lilacs in the spring and roses in the summer. He always has a joke or two, and a lot of them are Polish jokes. Since he's Polish, no one is offended.

"Did you hear about the Polish couple that got married and headed for Rochester on their honeymoon?" he asked.

"No." I always say no whether I did or not. I'm not about to ruin someone's day over a triviality.

"They were driving down the thruway, and the husband put his hand on his wife's thigh.

"We're married now, honey. You can go further," she said.

"So he drove to Syracuse."

Oh, Ernie, you bring your share of merriment.

May 23

It's funny how many old people don't want to take a bath or shower. I don't know why. Maybe they just don't want to have their comfort disturbed.

Lettie was one of these. She had been an army wife. Her husband was a career officer and had attained the rank of colonel. He died many years ago. An aide was preparing to give Lettie a bath. As she lowered her into the tub, Lettie said, "Goodbye, world."

The aide said, "You want to be clean for the colonel, don't you?"

Lettie answered, "The colonel wouldn't care, and if he knew what you were doing to me, he'd be here with half the army."

May 28

Something interesting happened to me that may be a valuable thing to know. About two months ago I cut back on my vitamin C intake. I figured if Rudy died before I do, it would be a little more difficult to get my herbs and vitamins since he buys them for me and gives me spending money besides. So I thought I'd practice cutting back and see how it worked out. (My kids would help but I'd rather be independent if I could.) So I cut my vitamin C intake from 1500 milligrams a day to 1000 milligrams a day.

Soon I started getting nosebleeds—what I consider bad ones. The blood would plop on my dress before I could feel it starting. It would take about twelve minutes to stop them. I got four or five in one month. When I saw our pharmacist I told him about it.

"Are you taking your vitamin C?" he asked.

I answered a simple yes, not wanting to go into my budgetary fears.

I upped my vitamin C intake to what it had been, and I've had no more nosebleeds. My daughter who's a nurse said that vitamin C strengthens the capillaries. The pharmacist said the same thing. I'm not suggesting that everyone who gets nosebleeds needs 1500 milligrams of vitamin C, because I think that I must have gotten my capillaries used to that dosage. I also think that we who have multiple sclerosis might need higher doses of vitamins than the general population.

May 29

Fred is one of our most handsome residents. He's well over six feet tall. He walks with a walker, but he stands straight and tall. His features are beautifully sculpted, and his bald head adds to, rather than detracts from, his attractiveness. I would say that, despite his eighty-nine years, he could be called a geriatric hunk. He was born in Arkansas and has retained his hillbilly accent, which gives him an "Aw, shucks" demeanor.

Every morning, around ten o'clock, he uses the public address system to give the time and temperature, to read a message from a magazine published for activity professionals, and then to sing a song *a cappella*, usually from the 1930s or 40s. His voice is a little gravelly, but he stays on key amazingly well.

I suppose if Fred can manage being "elderly" this gracefully, maybe I can too. But I think it's easier for men than for women.

7

The Aunt Janes

June 1, 1996

Aunt Jane, of whom I dreamed the nights it
thundered,
was dead at ninety, buried at a hundred.
We kept her corpse a decade, hid upstairs,
where it ate porridge, slept and said its prayers.
And every night before I went to bed
they took me in to worship with the dead.
Christ Lord, if I should die before I wake,
I pray thee, Lord, my body take.

—Alden Nowlan

ONE DAY I WAS LEAFING through an English Literature book
and came across this poem. It hit me with a poignancy
heightened by my residency here, where we have had many
Aunt Janes through the years.

I have lived in a four-bed room for the past thirteen years.
My present roommates are Joan, who is four years younger
than me, who is incapacitated by Parkinson's and arthritis, and
whom everybody adores, and Stephanie, a beautiful
107-year-old woman who is as alert as I am, and who is still
continent. She has lost some of her sight, but her hearing is still

good. The fourth bed, previously occupied by Lyd, the woman who had a feeding tube, is empty. When Lyd came back from the hospital, she had to have a room by herself because of Methicillin-resistant Staphylococcus aureus (MRSA), a very contagious staph bacterial infection.

But over the years I have had several Aunt Janes for roommates. They make wonderful roommates. Nothing you do bothers them because they're oblivious. I became very fond of some of them and of their families.

As you're growing up, your mother and your preacher admonish you to count your blessings. When you're young that sounds trite. You think the world is your oyster. But here the words come alive. If you have your sight and hearing and the use of your hands, you're wealthy. If your brain is functioning at full capacity, your cup runneth over. No, I take that back. You have to have verbal communication too.

Opal was one of those who had everything but verbal communication. She was two years younger than me and very intelligent. Amyotrophic lateral sclerosis, or ALS (Lou Gehrig's disease), was closing the muscles in her throat so that you had to listen closely to try to decipher the words she was trying to form. Try to talk with your mouth held open, and you'll see what I mean. It was very frustrating for her and for the listener if she had to repeat herself too often. She couldn't write because her hands were too contracted.

People avoided engaging her in conversations because of the difficulties. She came to activities, joining in everything anyway, and made everybody feel good just by her presence. She was a beautiful person with a lot of good stories to tell—we found out from her brother that she'd been to Europe twice and had won an automobile in a contest once—but her tongue was imprisoned in an uncooperative body. People with

ALS usually have a post-diagnosis life span of three to five years. Opal outlived that by about two years.

Sometimes I think God puts us in certain situations to teach us certain things. Most of us who are gathered under this roof can learn from one another. I think what he wants me to learn is patience. I can tell him right now it ain't workin'.

June 3

I got a letter from Dawn today. She was an aide here about eleven years ago. She now lives with her husband in Arizona. Oh, what memories. We are fugitives from justice together.

One morning on her day off she came bounding into my room and closed the door. "How can I get some nursing home stationery?"

"Why?" I asked.

She explained. She had gone downtown to the Social Services department to see about getting financial aid so she could continue her schooling to be a nurse. Her annual pay was four hundred dollars over the maximum to qualify. She said the clerk practically told her by innuendo that if she could falsify her salary on nursing home stationery, he would put the application through.

Well. I thought for a minute. I thought of all the possible abettors and rejected each one after only a moment's consideration. Finally I thought of Trish, the ward clerk. Perfect. I was pretty sure she'd have access to the stationery, and I was pretty sure she had enough devilry in her temperament to go along with a shady deal like that.

We looked her up and brought her into my room, and behind closed doors explained the dastardly deed we were contemplating. Trish is a very pretty, heavyset, middle-aged woman with an upsweep hairdo and a formidable bust line.

"Wait here," she said.

In five minutes she was back with two sheets of stationery tucked inside the pages of a policy booklet. Dawn typed the letter, and her friend, who had once been a nurse here, signed it. She got three thousand dollars to continue her education. It was the first time I've been involved in something illegal, and I loved it. If I hadn't gotten multiple sclerosis, I might have been in jail now instead of in a nursing home.

June 4 (Monday)

Thelma, one of our resident pinochle players, came down to the dining room for our afternoon pinochle session with tears streaming down her face.

"Whatever is the matter?" we wanted to know.

"My son-in-law was killed in a fire Saturday night."

Her daughter Heidi had already been widowed twice. About a year and a half ago, she married Chuck, a longtime friend. Thelma was very happy about it. She said the whole family loved Chuck.

Heidi and Chuck lived in a mobile home in a small town in Virginia. Last Saturday a noise woke them up in the wee hours of the morning. They both got up to investigate. The noise seemed to be coming from the direction of the freezer. When Heidi saw smoke coming from that area, she turned around toward safety, assuming Chuck would follow. But Chuck continued on to investigate, presumably hoping to put out the fire. He was overcome by smoke inhalation before help arrived. A neighbor, who pulled Heidi out through a window, saved her life. Thelma said it was the happiest of Heidi's three marriages, and now it had ended tragically.

June 7

We had the Volunteers Appreciation dinner last night. We have it every year to honor the volunteers who entertain us on a regular basis, laymen who lead our religious services, those who act as waiters and waitresses at our parties, and the former assistant director of nursing who does our mending. There are others, but I can't think of everyone right now. We usually have it in the backyard. We have a beautiful backyard—huge trees over or close to a hundred years old so there's always shade. This year the weather was threatening, so we had it in the dining room.

I'm always invited because I used to do the newspaper here, a fifteen pager. Now it's cut down to a mere few pages, more of a public relations vehicle, but I still help with it. I also sell the raffle tickets and football squares and candy bars to raise money.

One of the things on the menu was barbequed ribs. Wanda (activities director) and her husband make and sell barbeque sauce, and they used their sauce. It was the first time in my life I had ribs, and the sauce was out of this world. (I'm not fond of clichés, but that's what it was—just the right degree of spicy hot.) We also had chicken cordon bleu, which was a good thing because I'm really not crazy about ribs, except for that sauce.

June 8

I turned away from the supper table just as Cora was being wheeled out of the dining room.

"Hey," I hollered, "Cora's got my dress on." I buy most of my dresses from catalogues, so duplication was not likely.

When they undressed her, they found it was indeed my dress. I wash my own dresses in the bathroom sink every morning. I think it prolongs their lives. My dress must have been hanging in the bathroom, and Marian, one of our confused walkers, undoubtedly took it down and carried it over to north wing where it ended up in Cora's closet.

Cora has deteriorated in the last year, but she is one of our most mild-mannered members. She was only pleasantly confused when she came here. Her husband's name was Willie. He's been dead for many years. Cora spent much of her early time here waiting for Willie to pick her up or to meet her for lunch:

"Is Willie here yet?"

"Have you seen Willie?"

"Willie said he'd be here by five o'clock."

Usually someone responding, "Willie called and said he'd be a little late," or, "I'll let you know as soon as he gets here," would satisfy her for a while.

I have always felt it was too bad Cora never had any children because I think she would have made a lovely mother. I've never seen her lose her temper. Even when "they don't feed me," her protestations are low-key. She'll come into the dining room right after finishing a meal and want to know when she's going to eat. A cup of coffee and a cookie usually mollifies her but not always.

One day Margaret (the dietary supervisor) gave her a piece of chocolate pie. Cora ate the pie slice with gusto, then put her fork down and asked when she was going to be given something to eat.

"You just ate a piece of pie," Margaret said.

"I did not!" She was indignant.

"Cora," Margaret tried to explain, "there's the empty dish in front of you."

"That's not mine," she insisted.

When I tried to explain that she simply had forgotten, she accused me of lying, so Margaret gave her a second piece of pie with whipped cream and coffee. I'll have to remember Cora's tactic the next time dessert is really good.

There are times when Cora remembers that Willie is dead. She was having a conversation with Etta one night:

Cora: "My name is Cora."

Etta: "My name is Etta."

Cora: "Oh, is that your name, Nettie?"

Etta: "No, Etta"

Cora: "Oh, Etta."

Etta: "Yes, my granddaughter used to say to me, 'Gamma will you—'"

Cora: "Oh, is that your name, Nettie?"

Etta: "No, Etta."

Cora: "Oh, Etta."

Etta: "Yes, my granddaughter always said to me, 'Gamma did you—'"

Cora: "Oh, is that your name, Nettie?"

This went on for sometime. Then they got onto the subject of husbands. I heard Cora say, "When my husband died, a bunch of the fellows came around, but I didn't think it was right, right away. I waited a couple of months."

Why you little dickens, Cora.

8

You Gave Me a Bath like a Horse, You Pig!

June 10, 1996

YESTERDAY, RUDY AND I attended a surprise seventy-fifth birthday party at the Rod and Gun Club thirty-five miles away for the husband of Trish, the ward clerk who conspired in my illegal caper. There were men there who could transfer me from car to wheelchair and back, which is why I was able to go. There was a surprise for me too. Sharon, the girl who was the social worker when I was admitted to the home, was there. She now lives in Liverpool, New York, with her husband and daughter.

I haven't seen her in probably thirteen years. We got to reminiscing, of course, and one of our favorite memories was about a subject I mentioned earlier—someone who hated to take a bath. Sharon remembers it well.

An aide had just finished giving Eleanor a bath and was grooming her in her room. Sharon was showing relatives of a prospective resident through the facility. As she passed Eleanor's room she was hard put to keep her poise. The conversation went something like this:

Sharon: ". . . and these are our two-bed rooms . . ."

Eleanor: "She gave me a bath like a horse, that pig!"

Sharon: (trying to suppress her shock): ". . . and on this side are our three– and four-bed rooms . . ."

Eleanor: "Ya gave me a bath like a *horse*, ya pig!"

Sharon: (trying to ignore this humiliation): ". . . and down at the end . . ."

Sharon and the prospective clients were beyond earshot by the time Eleanor hollered, "I hope you smash your car up!"

Sharon didn't remember, but I'll bet that client chose our home. They probably had fewer regrets putting their loved one in our three-ring circus than in a nursing home.

June 12

Kate, our current social worker, came in this morning and told me Lyd died last night. Good for you, Lyd. They can take their nasogastric tube and stick it. You're free now. Thank you, God.

June 13

I'm frequently involved in the girls' (meaning the aides) problems. One was telling me some more today about her ongoing problem. She gave birth out of wedlock to a baby girl sixteen years ago. She also has three younger children by the man she married. Her firstborn's father, who lives out of state, has come back into the picture because his daughter by his present wife just died, and this aide thinks he is trying to replace the dead daughter by establishing contact with his first daughter. She resents this since he disappeared when she told him she was pregnant. She was telling me about the tongue-lashing she gave him on the phone yesterday: "and I just told him, Ya tore the f - - - - - - heart right outa my soul."

I've never heard it expressed so succinctly.

June 14

Edith was admitted to our facility today. She is
eighty-two years old and dying because of a brain tumor. Edith
lived three blocks from my house. She used to be my
hairdresser. I had to stop going to her when my condition made
it too difficult to walk those three blocks.

Her daughter used to be an aide here, one of the best we
ever had. Her granddaughters used to be good aides here too. It
was like a family reunion, seeing them again. We got caught up
with the news on each other's side of the fence.

Edith's prognosis is heartbreaking for them—as it would
be in any family—but Edith is a special person. Her
granddaughters were raised in a town about two hours away.
They moved in with Edith after high school because the job
market here was more promising. From then on, her modest
home on Pinecrest Drive was always open to any family
member who needed temporary or permanent refuge. She was
always the giver, the one people turned to in times of trouble.
And now she's dying of a brain tumor. Her dear ones have
difficulty accepting it.

Please, Lord, make it soon.

June 15

An aide and I were chatting. She is thirty-nine years old
and has a twenty-two-year-old son.

I said, "You were one of those teenage mothers that are
such a problem to society." (I did not say this harshly. It was in
a teasing tone.)

"Yes," she said. "But I was no problem. I got pregnant
when I was sixteen. My mother and my sister helped me raise
my son. He just graduated from Tuskegee Institute with an
accounting degree, and he's heavily into computers. He also

broke the record for track at Chestnut Hill High School when he was there."

"My nineteen-year-old daughter," she went on, "is entering State College this fall. My eighteen-year-old daughter is a senior in high school."

If everybody had a mother and sister like that, society wouldn't have a problem, would it?

June 18

The Group (our monthly lunch crew) celebrated Joan's seventy-second birthday at the Greek restaurant. There were ten of us. The daughter of a former resident who died a couple of years ago was here in the afternoon playing pinochle, so we asked her to come along. I doubt that there's any other nursing home in this area that has so many restaurants and a shopping plaza within wheelchair-pushing distance. It's a real bonus for those of us who can get out. But we usually go to the Greek restaurant because it's only one block away, and it has good food at reasonable prices.

We came back here and had the cake Rosalia baked. It was the best chocolate cake I've ever had outside of homemade. Box and commercial chocolate cakes are too light—a chocolate cake should be heavy—and the flavor isn't all that great. This was a box cake, but the recipe included chocolate pudding and chocolate chips, and I guess that's what made it heavy. It was great.

June 19

Terry (my friend whose granddaughter has MS) called. They stopped the Betaseron and started Robin on Avonex six days ago. This is another new medication for MS. The doctor feels it's more compatible with the body's own fluids than Betaseron.

June 20

We went to Margaret's retirement party at the Sarsparilla Room last night. She had just retired as the assistant food service manager. The twice-baked potatoes had the consistency of drying cement, and the apple-crisp ice cream had too many canned apples in ratio to the ice cream, but otherwise it was great. We sat with a fun group including Cindy and her husband Neal. I saw three people I hadn't seen in years, and all in all it was a lovely party.

Karen stopped in yesterday to give me a belated birthday present—a luncheon for Rudy and me. She used to work here. I haven't seen her in months. Her husband had a stroke, so she spends a lot of time with him. She also takes care of an elderly woman for three hours every morning, so her free time is limited. She was one of the ones I was very close to. I told her about the retirement party. She said they had her daughter's wedding reception there, and it sucked. I've never heard anything good about the place. I don't know how the Sarsparilla Room stays open.

June 26

Connie (an aide) told me an astonishing story this morning. Her fifteen-year-old daughter, Amanda, gave a pool party yesterday. Connie had bought contact lenses for Amanda, and one of them fell out in the four-foot deep, twenty-four-foot long pool. Connie debated on what to do—vacuum and sift through? Drain the pool? She finally decided. She had the girls form a circle and run inside the perimeter of the pool to create an eddy and cause everything to go to the center. Connie got a flashlight and studied the area in the center of the pool. She didn't really know what to look for because the lens was blue and the pool lining was blue.

After peering down into the water for close to an hour, she spied a tiny pinpoint that was darker blue than the rest of the pool. She moved her big toe over it and told Amanda to dive down and take whatever was under her big toe. Amanda came up with the lens.

I am so impressed by things I would be incapable of doing, and thinking of creating an eddy is one of them.

When Fred makes his ten o'clock public announcements, he often encourages us to stretch our minds. I sometimes wonder if my brain is like that old rubber band that breaks instead of stretches.

June 27

I rang to be taken off the bedpan at six thirty this morning. Ronnie answered the light. The first thing he did, of course, was make fun of my big butt. That's routine. I covered my face and began sobbing. He knew it was fake, of course.

He said, "What are you crying about? If you've got a big toucan, you've got a big toucan, and there's nothing you can do about it."

I think it would ruin his fun if I ever lost fifty pounds. Another aide, who is also black, says I have a fanny like a black woman's. She says it is bodacious. I looked that up in the dictionary. It means "splendid" or "showy." I either sit on it or lie on it twenty-four hours a day, which is a darn shame. Since it affords so much entertainment for those who do see it, it's too bad more people can't.

July 3

I was sitting at the table reading the newspaper after lunch. Dan, who is ambulatory in the feet but not in the head, was feeling my knee.

"Cut it out," I said—or something to that effect.

"Do you want me to come back later?" Dan asked.

"No, I don't," was my curt reply.

Mary Lou, a physical therapy aide, heard my tone of voice and gently escorted him out of the dining room. He turned to her and said, "She's a snappy bitch, ain't she?"

I passed Trixie in the hall wheeling her laundry cart a short time later, and I told her about the incident and Dan's remark.

"Well, you are," she said.

When Rosalia came in that evening, I told her.

Her response was, "Well you are, you know."

Geez!

July 8

Rudy and I were finishing eating supper on a picnic table in the backyard last night when Cindy, the Barbie doll housekeeper, came walking across the lawn. I was surprised, because she was operated on for a bowel obstruction a week ago. She lost ten pounds because she has no appetite. (I didn't either after my cholecystectomy—I think maybe the anesthesia changes your endocrine balance temporarily.) It had better be temporary. She can't afford to lose ten pounds.

Her absence has been so noticeable. She has a sense of humor that most people have to buy admission tickets to hear. I would share it with you, but much of it is in skit form that includes gestures and poses, so it's impossible to put on paper.

July 9

Rosalia came to work carrying a bag of homemade cheese rolls. She had made them from scratch this afternoon, and none of her family liked them. She loved them, but she was so disgusted with her family's attitude that she didn't want to look at them anymore. So she brought them in for Rudy and me because she knew we would eat anything.

July 10

I got a postcard from Pat LaPorta, our former director of nursing. She loves it in Arizona.

Too bad.

July 11

Sometimes my wheelchair leg supports don't click in place automatically. If the aide who dresses me forgets to click it manually, that leg support gradually swings outward. This was the case on Saturday morning. I was sitting by an activities room window in the late morning, reading one of my thrillers. Alice sat across from me. I don't know what her diagnosis is but she is what I call pleasantly confused. She asked me why I couldn't walk. I tried to explain to her that my brain sends the message to my legs to walk, but they don't get that message because it is ambushed on the way down the spinal cord. She just looked at me, and I had no idea how much her brain had absorbed.

During the next half hour, as I was reading, I could sense her studying me intently. Then she really caught my attention with, "I know why you can't walk. Your feet are too far apart."

Maybe the doctors should look into that.

9

The Maxi-Lift

July 15, 1996

THERE'S A SUBJECT I haven't touched upon because it's too painful. My weight. I must talk about it now because something happened that ticked me off, and I've got to let off some steam. I have gained about fifty pounds or more since I've been here. All my pre-MS adult life, I weighed 152 pounds. It was not overweight for me. I am five nine and large boned. I quit smoking in '71, gained a lot, dieted, and settled in at 164. Even that was not bad. Though I was wheelchair-bound and got no exercise, I was able to maintain that weight without giving up *all* the junk food.

When I came here I adhered to Adele's (the iridologist) program for two years. Then I began cheating by eating forbidden food. I cheated more and more over the years and gained more. For the last three years, I've been struggling to lose it. And I mean struggling. I've been able to discipline myself for three weeks tops, then something happens to break the pattern: a birthday party, a gift from someone "whose feelings I can't hurt," or a smorgasbord luncheon or something. Then I'm off my "diet."

Everyone has to get weighed once a month here. There's a good reason, of course. The nursing department has to know if someone is gaining or losing too fast. But I refuse to get

weighed because I don't want them to know how much I
weigh, and I don't want to know either. It's sort of a
hide-your-head-in-the-sand theory that I'm reluctant to give up.
(THE STATE supports me in this because I'm exercising my
patient rights.)

I have told myself all the advantages to losing weight:
becoming much easier to transfer, having more energy to do
everything, having better-fitting clothes. There are many more
advantages, but apparently this motivation isn't strong enough.
Mr. C. tells me periodically I look like a moose. (We have that
kind of relationship.) That hasn't motivated me either.

When I am tempted by candy or certain sweets, I adopt a
this-thing-is-bigger-than-both-of-us-so-why-fight-it mentality.
My latest attempt was skipping breakfast because if I eat
breakfast, my digestive system goes into gear too soon, and I
want to eat all day, especially after supper. That's only
successful sporadically because sometimes I'm hungry in the
morning. And much of the nutritional material I read says it's
important to eat breakfast. I have devised an eat-all-you-want
diet, but I haven't had the courage to try it yet. It's restricted to
Brussels sprouts, okra, and oysters. What really did me in was
selling Turtle Candies last year to raise money for the
resident's council fund. I can resist some candy bars, but not
Turtles (caramel and pecans dipped in chocolate). While I'm
vowing not to be sabotaged by this temptation, my arm works
independently of my brain. And the harder I keep vowing, the
faster my arm and mouth keep working.

I was recently made a "Maxi-Lift resident"—that's how
we word it—and it means the aides have to use a Maxi-Lift to
transfer me. It's like a Hoyer lift, but the design is different.
The aides can fit the sling around me while I'm already seated,
so I don't have to sit on it all day. It's kind of fun—like a
kiddie ride at an amusement park.

On Thursday, July 11, they couldn't find the sling when they were ready to transfer me. They searched every room, closet, laundry room, linen room, and every other nook and cranny over the next few days. Phyllis, a supervisor, called the commercial laundry to tell them to be on the lookout for it in case it had gone out with the sheets by mistake. I heard from confidential and reliable sources that Robert, an aide, told Ruth, another supervisor, that I didn't like the Maxi-Lift, and that I may have hidden the sling in my closet. I had said on more than one occasion that I thought the Hoyer lift was easier, but saying that I didn't like the procedure was not a true statement. It's time consuming, but that's the aides problem, not mine. Robert asked for my key on Friday so he could look in my closet. On Monday, Ruth asked for my key so *she* could search my closet.

I said, "Are you kidding?"

She said, "No, I'm not."

I told her Robert had searched it earlier, but I gave her the key. When she gave it back, she said it was just routine. Yeah, right.

I was perplexed. If I wanted to get rid of something, did they really think I'd hide it in my closet? In the first place, I didn't dislike the procedure. In the second place, it would be a very ineffective thing to do. It would be replaced in no time. In the third place, if I wanted to get rid of it—well, I wouldn't have given it to Rudy to take home although I heard that someone suggested I might have done that too—but I'm sure I could have thought of something more clever than hiding it in my closet.

July 17

The Maxi-Lift sling was shipped back this morning with the commercial laundry.

I'll never get an apology from Robert or Ruth because they both insisted their searches were routine although their attitudes suggested otherwise. And the implied accusation was insulting, not so much to my integrity as to my ingenuity. Closet. Really!

July 17, evening

Angeline is a four-foot-nine, eighty-six-year-old dynamo with the girth of a typical Italian mama. Angeline has three claims to fame. She has given birth to a dozen children, she has bounced back from the pronunciations of four last rites, and she closes each Catholic Alumni Club appearance with her rendition of "Show Me The Way To Go Home," a song the band played on her wedding night.

Her daughter Toni is a once– or twice-daily visitor. She is fifty-six years old, and she has a figure many thirty-year-olds would envy.

I was playing cards with my group at our regular dining room table. Toni was talking with a group of people at another table. She caught my attention when I heard her say, "Yes, I was married three times."

Gee, I thought, I didn't know that.

She went on. "My first husband died of eating poisoned mushrooms."

Wow!

"And my second husband died of eating poisoned mushrooms," she continued.

Having had the experience of writing the nursing home newspaper, my journalistic instincts went on immediate alert. What a great biography this would make!

Then came the kicker. "My third husband died of a fractured skull. He wouldn't eat the poisoned mushrooms."

Everybody's laughter was explosive, but none so much as mine, which acknowledged my gullibility and my incredulity at having been duped. If laughter is the best medicine, I still get a good healing dose now and then. Thanks, Toni.

July 18

The pattern of visitations among our residents' loved ones is odd. There are some spouses or children, like Toni, who come every day, some who come three or four times a week, some who come about once or twice a week—even though their loved ones don't know them. Then there are the others—the ones who come three or four times a year. I don't understand it. I'm thinking of two daughters in particular whose mothers have some type of dementia. They probably don't know their daughters any longer, but they both have beautiful dispositions—no belligerence—so I don't imagine it would be too unpleasant to visit them. I'm quite sure both daughters work, so that cuts down on available time. But three or four times a year for a family that lives nearby? I don't understand it.

I was sitting in the doorway of my room after lunch waiting for two aides to be available to toilet me. Louisa lives in the room across the hall from me—she has a gentle disposition. She told me how pretty my dress was. I thanked her.

"That fan down the hall is terrible," she said.

"Oh, really?" I replied. "I like it."

"It musses my hair up, and I don't think we need it. It's a nice day."

"It's a beautiful day," I said, agreeing.

"My cousin took me for a ride in the country," she said.

"You mean yesterday?"

"No, today."

I knew this wasn't true, and I realized for the first time that she wasn't as lucid as she had seemed to me from our usual short conversations. But I said, "Oh, that must have been wonderful."

"Yes it was. He wanted to stop and have lunch, but I had already eaten."

"Why didn't you eat again anyway?" I asked.

"I never thought of that. You always think of the right things when it's too late."

"The next time, tell him to let you know beforehand so you can skip lunch."

"That's a good idea," she agreed. "I'm going to do that."

It wasn't until this conversation that I realized the nature of Louisa's disability. Her brain cells were deteriorating apparently in just the right place to allow her to invent adventures or recall memories that were as pleasurable to her now as if she were actually experiencing them in the present. If a dementia is your lot in life, that's a great pattern of brain cell deterioration rather than one that induces belligerence or paranoia or anxiety.

July 21

One of our maintenance men got married yesterday. Short and bearded, he has a booming voice. Whatever he does—buff the floors, mow the lawn, shovel the snow—he does with gusto.

Paula was one of the guests. She has been the head of our dietary department for fifteen years. Paula is a little on the heavy side, but she has a beautiful face. She's sixty-two years old, and she's been divorced since 1981. We—and she's included in the we—do a lot of teasing about her finding another husband. I have it on good authority that just as the bride threw the bouquet at the reception, Paula bellowed, "Out of my way," and with arms outspread made a successful lunge for it.

If she ever gets married, it's going to spoil a whole lot of fun for a whole lot of people, including her.

July 25

My dear friend Vicky and her husband Dave arrived in Buffalo on the twenty-third for a visit. Vicky and I met at the school-bus stop in 1956, right after Rudy and I had moved our family into her neighborhood. We were each waiting for the bus with our kindergartners. As we walked back to our respective houses, Vicky said, "I'll invite you in for coffee as soon as my son is over scarletina." She did. That was the beginning of a friendship that included daily phone chats, frequent luncheons, and poker sessions with our husbands and her parents. Her need to work after her divorce curtailed much of our contact, but it didn't dilute our friendship.

When Vicky remarried, she and Dave moved from Buffalo to Arizona. They now live in Asheville, North Carolina, which they consider a nice compromise between Arizona's sweltering summers and Buffalo's harsh winters. They get to Buffalo once a year, and we keep in touch through letters and phone calls.

Vicky is nine years younger than me, and she has not aged a whole lot since I met her. Her hair is a darker blonde now, but she still has the beautiful features and luminous blue eyes that made her so pleasant to look at years ago. Dave is a good mate for her. He is still good looking, even though he is seventyish and he has a laid-back temperament that undoubtedly contributed to his success in the business world.

Since they've been here, it's been a whirlwind three days of lunches and crazy rummy—or contract rummy—or whatever some people call it. That particular card game contributes a lot toward keeping my humility level high. It's a version of rummy, but it's very structured, with certain rules that make it very tense.

Dave and I were partners, and we ended up breaking even after three days, but that was due almost solely to Dave's shrewdness. It's well known that I'm lucky at cards, and this has held true through the years. But this session was too much for me. Even Dave, who is ordinarily thoughtful and considerate, was driven to say, "You know, I think you're a liability." I could probably forget this humiliation if this were the end of it till another year. But it's not. My daughter, Kathy, and her husband John will be here in two weeks, and I'll have to face the possibility of the same disgrace all over again.

July 26

Rosalia came in unexpectedly today to oversee the activities department. She was filling in for the regularly scheduled girl, who had something important to attend. Rosalia brought some microwave popcorn with her. I pigged out.

July 28

My grandson Joe and his girlfriend were due to arrive at Rudy's house early yesterday afternoon. Joe is completing his first year residency in pharmacy at the VA Hospital in

Gainesville, Florida. His girlfriend Jean (Great name—I like her already!) has two years of study left to get her Pharm D. (pharmacy doctorate) in the same program. Their plans were to fly to Cleveland, rent a car, and drive to Cedar Point, Ohio, for a day of thrills on the rides. Their next stop would be Buffalo for a visit with Rudy and me.

Rudy came over to the nursing home at noon yesterday. He was upset. "I've been up all night waiting for them, and they haven't showed yet," he said. "Joe called last night about nine thirty, and said he'd drive straight through."

Rudy has some hearing loss. He wears hearing aids but still misses words here and there in a conversation, even when it isn't over the phone.

"You probably didn't get the whole conversation," I suggested.

"No," he insisted, "that's what Joe said: 'We'll drive straight through.'"

We talked it over, and I ended up calling the State Trooper station in Clarence, New York, to see if they could check the accident reports along whatever route is the main route between here and Cedar Point. They referred me to the Amherst Police, hung up, and probably laughed themselves silly. I called the Amherst Police, who referred me to the State Troopers in Clarence. *They* hung up and probably laughed themselves silly. I called Joe's brother Curt, in Daytona Beach. Fortunately, he had forgotten to give me his new unlisted telephone number. I called his mother Kathy in Daytona Beach. Fortunately, she wasn't home. We finally decided there was nothing to do but wait. I tried to adopt a casual attitude, but my stomach made it difficult.

Joe and Jean arrived at Rudy's around one thirty. I asked Joe what he had said.

He said, "I said maybe we'd drive right through."

Aaah! That little word "maybe." What a difference that one little word can make. I have coined a maxim: As you go through life, look for those "maybes" before you go bonkers.

10

Death Comes in Threes

July 27, 1996

I READ SOMETHING in Dear Abby's column yesterday that moved me and gave me a sense that the writer shares my feelings about death and dying. It's titled, "What Is Dying" by Luther F. Beecher.[2]

> I am standing upon the seashore. A ship at my side spreads her white sails to the morning breeze and starts for the blue ocean. She is an object of beauty and strength, and I stand and watch until at last she hangs like a speck of white cloud just where the sun and sky come down to meet and mingle with each other. Then someone at my side says, "There! She's gone!" Gone where? Gone from my sight—that is all. She is just as large in mast and hull and spar as she was when she left my side and just as able to bear her load of living freight to the place of destination. Her diminished size is in me, not in her.

> And just at the moment when someone at my side says, "There! She's gone!" there are other eyes watching her coming and other voices ready to take up the glad shout, "There she comes!"

> And that is—"dying."

When someone dies here, we don't often say, "I'm sorry" to the families of those who died. We say, "God, I'm going to miss her," or "I'm glad he's gone; he suffered so." Sometimes, among ourselves, we say, "What a relief. She sure was a pain in the ass."

We do a lot of thinking about immortality here—or rather about mortality. We have a saying: death comes in threes. Sometimes we have to condense the calendar to fit three deaths into one time frame, but in general that's about how it works out. When two die, we wait expectantly until the third one goes, wondering "Will it be me?" Most of the time it's someone who's been ill in bed for a couple of weeks or more. But sometimes it happens suddenly. We know our turn is coming. Sometimes at night when I'm tired and discouraged I say, "Please, God, take me now. I'm ready." In the morning when I'm refreshed, I say, "Well, God, I wouldn't mind a little more time."

I wanted to give my organs for transplant (I once read that even kidneys from very old people are useful for transplant if they're in good condition), but I was told that organs from someone with a disease like mine are unacceptable for transplant. I think that's kind of dumb. I'd rather have a subpar heart or liver from an MS patient than none at all.

I'm still trying to decide about leaving my body for dissection by our university students. Maybe I'll let my kids make the decision. Well, anyway, a parable on death and dying shrinks the ego and helps to put death in a proper perspective.

Speaking of mortality, now is the time to tell you about Josie. I'm more worried about Josie's mortality than I am about my own. I can't imagine living here without her. Everybody loves her. Josie is of Italian descent. She has short clipped white hair, a lovely shaped generous nose, and a smile that lights up a room. She walks all day—up and down the south wing, up and down the north wing, into the dining room, and around the activities room. She "washes" the walls vigorously with her hands and smooths out imaginary sheets on the tables.

She picks up all things that aren't nailed down and sticks them under her sweatshirt. I don't know when she eats because she often walks among the tables while we're eating. But she isn't losing any weight in spite of the exercise she gets, so I know she eats.

When I was writing the newspaper here, I did one-page biographies of many of the residents and some of the staff. I got most of the information from the residents' families. I wanted to do Josie's biography, but one of her sisters said "no." She said her life was too tragic to have it documented. Josie's smile indicates that, whatever was in her past, she's happy now. Sometimes something happens, probably in her mind, that angers her, and she will bawl me out indignantly. "You—you—you—you—you," she will stutter, followed by a string of epithets understood by only her. Her tongue-lashings, accompanied by flashing eyes and a reprimanding finger, are funny because they're unjustified, and I have to clench my fists to keep from laughing. My "I'm sorry, I'm sorry, I won't do it again" usually fails to mollify her, but eventually she turns away and is in good spirits again.

One day last week Josie came over and stood by my table while I was eating lunch. I had a bowl of watermelon for dessert. I speared a piece with my table knife, which I hadn't used, and put it in her mouth. Her face took on the expression of a one-year-old discovering ice cream.

"Is it good?" I asked.

"Uh-huh," she said, nodding. Her eyes twinkled.

I wanted to give her more, but her attention span is too short. She was gone. How can an eighty-year-old woman, who is so hunchbacked that it's anatomically difficult for her to look up, whose attention you can't get because her dementia has progressed too far, and who speaks nothing but gibberish if she speaks at all, capture your heart? It has happened here.

July 29

Yesterday Tracey, a south wing aide, brought me some spaghetti salad her mother had made. I've been hearing about spaghetti salad for a year, but I've never had the opportunity to taste it. It was wonderful. It was spicy hot, and I love spicy hot. Her mother put in tomatoes, green peppers, and onions, diced fine. She mixed it with Italian dressing and hot seasoning. It's eaten cold, of course. You can put in any vegetables you want, and you don't have to have it spicy hot, but I liked it just the way Tracey's mother made it.

August 5

We got a new roommate today to fill the bed vacated by Lyd. She's eighty-four or eighty-six years old, and her name is Rose. She has Lou Gehrig's disease. She's confused and wonders why she's here. I can't possibly know how she feels because I came voluntarily. A family member placed her here because she could no longer be taken care of at home. Her speech is affected, as was Esther's, who died here of the same disease. You can barely understand her now, and I know what's coming.

Dear God, how are these people chosen—these people who have to suffer so before they die? I am so lucky to have so many capabilities left.

August 8

My daughter Kathy and her husband, John, arrived in Buffalo about six o'clock, I guess. Rudy and I weren't here. We were stranded down at the Greek restaurant. Our luncheon group had gone there for supper. Five of us had walked down from the nursing home. The rest drove. When it was time to leave it was pouring rain. We stood on the outside stoop people-watching for three quarters of an hour before it stopped. People watching isn't such a bad pastime.

Kathy and John were lucky. It was hot and muggy the day before their arrival, but the weather was gorgeous all the while they were here. Kathy is my second oldest daughter, the mother of my two grandsons. At forty-seven she is still attractive. Her five-foot-eight frame is topped by curly, honey-blonde hair that falls just below the shoulders. John's features are nice enough to make him handsome. He was born and raised in Florida and has a slight southern drawl. I once saw a cushion embroidered "Happiness is being married to your best friend." I think this is Kathy and John.

August 12

Kathy and John left this morning, and I'm wallowing in the letdown feeling you have after company leaves. I will feel abandoned for most of the day.

My card-playing luck was worse than I had predicted. John and I were partners. The last two days we broke even, but we never recouped the three dollars we lost the first day. John is a master at saving a person's self-esteem. He left a letter for me that read in part:

> You have been a good partner at cards. We got lousy cards the whole time, but thanks to our high skill levels we were able to convert the lousiest cards into something workable and at times, true masterpieces.

Nice try, John.

On top of that, the ambience Joan, Stephanie, and I have created in our room is not compatible with our new roommate's temperament, physical condition, or emotional needs. Rose cannot tolerate a TV set being on. Joan uses hers as a soporific. Rose cannot stand my light being on, even though the curtain between us is pulled. If I can't watch TV, I like to read. But she won't allow either. And when I say "won't allow," I mean she doesn't let up. I don't think we can tolerate a new resident coming into this room and dictating how we should live. Rose has to go.

August 15

Rose was awake at five this morning doing her thing. She kept all of us awake. Besides her hollering, her bed alarm is very screechy, and she sets it off constantly. A bed alarm is put on some beds to alert the staff when residents who need help try to get out of bed on their own. Rose has a feeding tube in her abdomen, so she has to have an aide go with her to move the pole that holds the pump when she wants to walk.

I know I'm cranky from lack of sleep, but Rose really should be in a room with comatose residents. I spoke to Kate (social worker) last Monday. She indicated something would be done.

August 16

We had our annual picnic yesterday. It was great as usual. Every year, in July or August, we invite our families to come for the afternoon to this festive occasion. The backyard is decorated with balloons hanging from the trees and from the ramp railings. We usually have a live band, but this year the entertainers—an exceptional and very dynamic husband and wife singing team—brought a sound system. Their repertoire ran from the Golden Oldies to a selection from *Phantom of the Opera.*

We always have a theme: German, Hawaiian, the Circus, and so on, and some of the staff wear coordinating costumes. The dietary staff devises menus that are compatible with the theme. This year the theme was baseball. Everybody who owned a baseball cap wore it, including the guests. We had a popcorn machine, a peanut stand, a cotton candy machine, and an ice cream stand. Everything was free, of course. I loved the menu: fresh fruit cup, beef on weck (roast beef on a kummelweck roll), sausages, hot dogs, potato salad, pasta salad, baked beans, and apple pie. The salads were exceptionally good. They didn't have too much mayonnaise in them, just enough to hold them together. That's my criterion for a good salad—as little mayonnaise as possible.

There was a lot of impromptu dancing too. Rebecca, an activities aide, led some of the staff in the Electric Slide and the Macarena. Sean, one of the south wing aides, did the Twist all the way down the walkway while he was passing out beer and pop to the guests. I've never seen more rhythm, even in a professional entertainer.

Some of the sons and daughters or spouses of former residents who died here come to this affair, so there is a lot of kissing and hugging—kind of like a family reunion. To top it off, the weather was superb. Rudy and I always sit under one of the big old trees. The picnic is one of the things I really look forward to each year.

August 17

I was having trouble with my printer, so I called Gayle yesterday. Gayle has been a wonderful friend to me since I met her about thirteen years ago, shortly after I moved into the nursing home. She is not much more than fifty. She was born in Australia. She came to Canada in 1965, and then moved to the United States in 1971. She's been gone from Australia for thirty-one years, but she has retained her charming accent. Her natural beauty doesn't require makeup. She has what I call a pixie haircut (short and uneven), which contributes to her girlishness.

Gayle and I met when she called the multiple sclerosis society to say she was especially interested in diseases of the central nervous system and would like to visit someone on a volunteer basis. My MS counselor happened to answer the phone, and she gave Gayle my name. Our relationship became that of friends rather than volunteer and resident. She has taken me on many nice outings.

Gayle is a midwife (not active at present). She was working at our nearby university in a research program, and she was studying for a doctorate in linguistics when I met her. About six or seven years ago I bought a computer, and Gayle taught me how to use it. She's the one I turn to in times of computer trouble. My way of attacking problems is, "Oh, damn" or "Oh, shit," and then, "That son-of-a-bitchin thing." Gayle's way is, "Hmmm, we have a problem here. Lets see how we can go about this logically." She once attended a problem-solving class. Maybe that gives her an edge.

We think she found the problem—the printer kept saying, "add paper" even though there was paper in it. Gayle thinks the tension was too tight (it has a tractor feed), and she said to keep giving it more slack. I haven't had a chance to test it because Gayle took the first nine chapters of this "tome" home to print on her printer.

August 18, morning

We almost had a crisis but it was averted. Helga, our little Norwegian nurse, came into my room to warn aides

Tracey and Yvette that Ray had crawled into Gretchen's bed
for a nap after Gretchen had gone to the dining room for
breakfast. Helga couldn't get him out—but eventually Sean,
one of our male aides, did.

Gretchen is my next-door neighbor, a large-built, pleasant
German woman who speaks with a Czechoslovakian-German
accent. She's about eighty-six years old, and rumor has it that
she was mugged and pushed down a flight of stairs in New
York City about two years ago, right before she came here. Her
voice is exceptionally high-pitched, and when she is agitated it
becomes very shrill. Rumor also has it that this is the result of
an operation that was necessary because of the mugging.

She is very solicitous of my roommate Stephanie (who is
107 today—our records show 103, but she insists it's 107).
Right before Gretchen goes to bed, when she and Stephanie are
sitting outside their rooms, she will wheel about eight feet
down the hallway and say to Stephanie, "Are you feeling *vell*?"
Stephanie assures her she is. Then Gretchen says, "All right, I
vill check on you again before I go to bet."

Gretchen likes to go to bed right after supper. The aides
have to clear the dining room before they can start putting
people to bed. They explain this to Gretchen, but her patience
has run out by the end of the day, and her voice becomes
almost unbearably shrill. If she had come back from breakfast
and found Ray in her bed she would have gone through the
roof and taken everyone within a thirty-foot radius with her.
I'm ashamed to admit I was kind of looking forward to it, but
Sean got him out and ruined my diabolical idea of fun.

Speaking of Stephanie, I asked her son about the
discrepancy our records show for her age. He said that years
ago people took four or five years off their ages when applying
for insurance polices. It made the premiums lower. She was
advised to do this by her insurance agent. But Stephanie says

she had her son when she was twenty-three and he is now
eighty-four, so this makes her 107. I really could have asked
her instead of Leo. She has no degree whatever of senility.
She's a small Polish woman with lovely features. She's still
continent. What genes to pass on to her descendants!

August 18, evening

Hallelujah. They moved Rose to another room where the
other resident is in a stupor and won't even notice her noise
making. Thank you, Kate.

11

Judge Crater, Call Your Office

August 19, 1996

I REALLY HAVEN'T TOLD YOU YET about Mr. Castellana, our administrator. I told you he's Italian and good-looking. He just turned sixty-one years old. His hairline has receded far enough to make a deep salt-and-pepper fringe around his head. Within the past year he has grown a mustache to match. (The jury's still out on that one.) His generous black eyebrows have no hint of gray, and maybe that's what it is that gives him a look of authority.

When I first came here, there were a few incidents that made me realize he's a no-nonsense guy. A resident in the room next to mine had a pale blue African violet. Pale blues are sometimes hard to get. The resident was confused and, I thought, undoubtedly she didn't care what color it was, if she even noticed. I wheeled up to the nurse's station where four staff members had gathered—three old-timers and one new, rigid supervisor whom we called "The Sergeant" behind her back.

I asked the group, "Do you think it would be okay if I traded one of my African violets for that blue one that Mrs. Whomever has? I'm sure she wouldn't know the difference."

Florence, one of our most caring nurses, said, "Why don't we ask her."

Boy, that was a solution that I'd never thought of. So Florence wheeled me into her room with one of my full blooming violets in my hand. Florence introduced me and explained to Mrs. Whomever that I had an African violet that I wanted to exchange with hers because I liked the color of hers. Hers was no longer in bloom, so I guess she considered that a good bargain. She readily agreed.

The next morning Mr. C. sent a message down to my room that he'd like to see me in his office. That sounded ominous. I went down as soon as I was dressed. He wheeled my chair in and closed the door. Then he sat down behind his desk and leaned back. I had no idea what was coming. He started out with something like, "You must understand that when people enter this facility, it is my responsibility to protect their property."

I looked at him quizzically. Then, I can't remember his exact words, but they were something like, "It has been reported to me that you took a plant from the woman in the room next to you."

I told him exactly what had happened. He looked skeptical. He wouldn't tell me who had reported it but I knew none of the old-timers would have, so it had to be The Sergeant.

He said, "Who was the nurse who took you into the room?"

I gave him Florence's full name. He said, "All right," as if he were going to check my story with her (he never did), and that was the end of the conversation.

Afterwards, I thought I should have told him, "Tell The Sergeant for me to get her facts straight before she runs to tattle." Not that he would have, but I would have liked him to know that I knew who the reporter was. The denouement of this tale is that, when my newly acquired violet finally bloomed, it was deep purple. Somebody had beaten me to the switch.

There were other occasions when Mr. C. had to call me into his office to ask me about something, but I can't think what the occasions were. I don't know why I remember this one so well and can't think of any of the others. It must be that I still feel some guilt about the others and want to forget them. Anyway, I finally told him that I'd like to do any talking in the dining room instead of his office. It would make me feel less like an errant adolescent.

Mr. C. is a laid-back kind of person. He's not an administrator who stays in his office. He's easy to talk to, and he's available. Over the years our relationship has grown into one of friendly mutual harassment. He treats me like a peer rather than a nursing home resident, and I'm grateful for that. Somewhere along the way, he became "Doug" much more frequently than "Mr. C."

Two years ago he took me to a dinner honoring a member of the New York State Department of Health. He had purchased two tickets and our Director of Nursing couldn't go at the last minute because of a family emergency, so he invited me to use her ticket. He introduced me to all the nursing home bigwigs as "the only date I could get who can't get away from me."

I enjoy teasing him too. Frequently, if we are playing pinochle with only three players, he will push up a stool and say, "Hurry up, I've got time for one game."

A few weeks ago during one of these sessions, something came out in the conversation about him being out of town for a few days. Then the conversation went something like this:

Me: "Where are you going?"

Doug: "None of your business."

Me: "What's that got to do with it? I want to know where you're going."

Doug: "I'm not going to tell you."

Me: "I'll start a nasty rumor about you."

Doug: "Like what?"

Me: "That you're sleeping with Kate [the social worker]."

Doug: "Hmm-m-m, that's not a bad idea. Ask her for me."

It's hard to get the best of him, but I keep trying. I must succeed in some fashion, because before he leaves the table, he usually tells me what I want to know.

Therese is Doug's assistant. Wanda is the activities director. Margo is the owner. The reason I mention all three at once is because they have so much in common. They're all attractive, petite, and dress as if they were coached by Oleg Cassini.

Margo's outstanding attribute is a voice so low and husky it could seduce a beefeater while he's on guard duty at the Tower of London. She's an avid reader, as I am, so we often exchange books or, if we don't have them, tell each other which ones to get.

The thing I admire most (and envy) about Wanda, besides her expertise as an activities director, is her waistline. I think if I put both my hands around her waist, my fingers and thumbs would touch. Her energy is boundless. The barbeque sauce she and her husband make and sell is receiving great acclaim. When their customer list gets long enough, she may leave here to devote full time to it.

Therese has more to her credit than her physical attributes. She is a kind and compassionate person—except once when I regarded her as an ogre. It was January 25, 1990. We were in the process of redecorating. The corridors and the dining and activities rooms were completed. The workmen were coming that evening to tear off the wallpaper in the lobby. I took the opportunity to do something I'd wanted to do for years—smear some graffiti around. I got a magic marker, and on the main wall of the lobby I wrote: "*Cognito, ergo,* spud—I think, therefore, I yam." Then I wrote in big letters my all-time favorite piece of graffiti: "Judge Crater, call your office."

Fran, the evening receptionist, was sitting at her desk a few feet away from me. As I was finishing up, her phone rang. Her end of the conversation went something like this: "Uh-huh . . . Oh . . . Oh . . . Uh-huh . . . Well, okay, I'll leave a note for Therese."

She hung up and said, "Jean, that was one of the men who are going to tear the paper off the lobby. They won't be able to come tonight because the weather is too bad."

"WHAT?" My heart fell down to my stomach. I think all the blood left my face. "Oh my God, Fran, what will I do?"

She shrugged as if she didn't know.

"Do you think we should call Therese?" I asked.

"Well, I think we should, but I don't really like to bother her at home."

"Yeah," I felt the same way, but I couldn't imagine her walking into a graffiti-infested lobby with no forewarning.

"Oh, my God, Fran, what am I going to do?"

She didn't seem able to come up with a solution. "I could call Therese at home, but—I don't know . . ."

I don't think I would have been more horrified if I had just found out my house had burned down.

I agonized for another minute, my mind racing desperately for a way to explain this to Therese. I wanted to die—anything to get out of this situation that I had stupidly created. The thought even crossed my mind of enlisting Fran's cooperation in pretending she didn't know who did it. But I dismissed it immediately. That wouldn't work.

I agonized out loud. "Oh, my God." The kind, compassionate woman had been transformed in my mind into a stern disciplinarian.

Fran must have decided I had suffered enough. She burst into laughter and said, "That wasn't the men. It was Trixie."

Trixie (who works in the laundry) was working as an evening activities aide at that time. She happened to glance out at the lobby and saw what I was doing. Then she cooked up the plot and called Fran.

The men took the paper off, of course, but somebody saved it and showed it to Therese and Doug anyway. That's the reason I know the exact date. The next day I was handed a letter on Nursing Home embossed stationary that read:

Dear Mrs. Misura:

Writing on the walls of the Amherst Nursing and Convalescent Home, even in jest, is an automatic discharge to another facility. (Policy # 7A Para. 3)

You have been duly noted as one who has defaced our walls. You, therefore, are ordered to pack up all of your JUNK.

We would suggest that you begin packing immediately, given the amount of accumulation you have. If you require assistance with this transfer, our social worker will assist you with moving to another facility or becoming a bag lady.

It was signed by both Doug and Therese. When I came to the word JUNK I knew for sure that it was a joke. The harassment continues. It goes both ways and adds zest to my life.

August 19, evening

We had such excitement this afternoon. First we had another crisis with Gretchen, the screamer who lives in the next room. Carol, the former navy nurse, took Gretchen's hospital table to another room for someone to use while he was eating. Gretchen was very upset. She told me they moved everything out of her room. Carol tried to explain that the table wasn't hers; it belonged to the nursing home, and they had to borrow it occasionally. She said Gretchen could have it back when they were through (even though Gretchen doesn't use it). This did not appease her. Gretchen is truly a lovely person, but if she lived next door to St. Peter he would have to keep an aspirin bottle handy for the times when she gets agitated.

Then, Helga, our little Norwegian nurse, came down to the dining room about three o'clock, just as we were about to start our card game.

"You won't believe it," she said. "Stella just responded to stimuli."

Our response was predictable: "WHAT?"

Stella fell down her stairs several months ago. The result was some broken bones and a coma. Today, Helga was sitting in the nurses' station. The call light from Stella's room went on. Helga thought an aide must have brushed against it and went in to check. Stella was squeezing it with her hand. Helga thought maybe her hand had found it by accident. She put it on Stella's chest and walked out. Immediately it went on again. Helga went back in and said, "Stella, squeeze my fingers if you can hear me." Stella squeezed her fingers.

Then Helga said, "Stella, kick your right leg." Stella's right leg went back and forth.

Helga called Carol, and Stella did the same things for her. They called Phyllis, the supervisor, and Stella responded the same for her, even opening her eyes when Phyllis asked her. This is after five months in a coma. There has been nothing since, but not even twenty-four hours has gone by.

The activities magazine messages that Fred read over the public address system this morning mentioned the importance of remaining thankful for the small things. Well, I'm thankful Stella was able to connect with another human being after so long. Her miracle today reminds me of Glen and Sarah.

Glen was one of the alumni who came to the picnic. He stops in every now and then, and we're thankful for that too. We want to remain in touch. Glen's wife Sarah died here two years ago. Sarah was beautiful, inside and out. She had fine features and a head full of beautifully coiffed gray hair. She was in her seventies and just a tad on the plump side. She wore makeup, jewelry, and perfume, and her wardrobe was such that she always looked as if she were going out for the evening. It was a simple delight just to look at her sitting across the room.

She had many physical problems, including strokes, which robbed her of speech and the ability to walk. We lovingly called her "Lala" because that's all that came out when she tried to speak.

Sarah was involved in a minor miracle like Stella's. One day I was sitting next to Sarah in the lobby, and I was selling raffle tickets for the bears Penny's mother had made. As Trixie passed with the laundry cart, I took the opportunity for a little hard sell.

"Aren't you going to buy yet?" I asked.

"Oh, I keep forgetting to bring the money," Trixie said.

"Write it down," said Sarah, clearly enough to be distinguishable. It was the first she had spoken in several years. It never happened again, but it made everyone feel elated for the rest of the day.

August 20

Tested the printer. It still doesn't work. I'll have to resort to "*Oh, shit!*" and "*Oh, damn.*"

August 21

Kim (the little Vietnamese girl who wants to bring her parents and sister here) told me this morning that her mother and father will have to get a divorce. It doesn't look as if her father will get an early release, and her mother will not be able to leave Vietnam while she's associated with Kim's father. They will remarry if Kim ever gets them both over here. The amount of paper work is tremendous.

She went into the bathroom and flushed the toilet. "That is disgusting," she said.

"What?" I asked.

"When someone dumps a bedpan and doesn't flush the toilet."

"Do they have flush toilets in Vietnam?" I asked. I am very ignorant about cultures of other countries. I do a lot of reading, but not much that's educational.

"The houses in the cities do, but not in the villages." She went on. "My parents' house has a flush toilet but not my grandparents'. In the villages they have a seat built over a pond, and the fish eat the feces."

"WHAT?"

She giggled at my dismay. "You can see the fish jumping up to catch the poop."

Besides being amazed, I was puzzled. "Do they have only one seat?"

"No, they have four. The toilets are a slab of wood with four holes. They're held in place by crisscross slats of wood anchored in the bottom of the pond," she explained.

"How do you get out to it? Is there a bridge?" I asked.

"Yes, you walk on wooden planks."

"It's not enclosed?"

"There's a low wall around the seat built of split coconut leaves that have been sewn together. That's all."

"Do four people ever use it at once?"

"Oh, sure," she said.

I giggled at the picture this created in my mind.

"It was about a quarter or a half mile from my grandparents' house," she added. "When I needed to go at night, I had to cut through the cemetery. It was scary."

While I was trying to digest this information, she gave me more to chew on. "Some people caught the fish and ate them, but we didn't."

"What kind of fish were they?"

"I don't know. I think catfish."

"What are the houses made of?" I asked.

"In the city, same like here. Our house was made of brick. But in the villages, coconut leaves. The kitchen is a separate building—away from the house. That's so if it catches on fire the whole house won't burn down. The weather is so hot and dry, it's easy to catch on fire."

Someone needed Kim to help with another resident, so that ended the conversation. But I think the fishpond toilets are one of the most amazing things I've heard about any culture.

How would I have learned about those amazing toilets if I had stayed stuck in a bed, isolated in my own little home, waiting for someone to come empty my bedpan?

12

Hello, Police?

August 22, 1996

I HAVE A TERRIBLE HABIT. When they're playing Trivia in the activities room, I have a compulsion to answer—with the wrong answers. The front half of the activities room is separated from the dining room where we play cards by two wide archways, one open and the other with a half wall, on which rests our hundred-gallon aquarium. I face the activities room while we're playing, so I get peripheral enjoyment from the activities. But when it's Trivia or a crossword puzzle, my enjoyment becomes active.

When playing Trivia, it goes something like this: Rebecca, who is on staff, stands in front of a group of residents and says, "What was the name of the Indian princess who saved John Smith?"

I shout something like, "Running Water."

Rebecca usually ignores me but Cliff, one of our residents, laughs.

Rebecca is one of our beautiful activities aides. She has mahogany skin, molded-to-the-head black hair, and fine features. She's about fifteen pounds too heavy to be called slender, but she's built solid and carries it with grace. And she has a singing voice that is more beautiful than many of the professionals we hire to entertain.

Today, Rebecca asked, "A tool used to drive nails is called a . . . ?"

I shouted, "Monkey wrench."

Cliff laughed and a few others tittered.

After she got the right answer from someone, Rebecca went to the next card, "In 1912 the British steamer Titanic sank because it hit an . . . ?"

I shouted the first thing that came into my mind. "Apple tree!" I got a lot of laughs from that one.

After someone answered "iceberg," Rebecca asked, "If you were in a boat and wanted to stay in one place, what would you put over the side?"

"The captain," I yelled. Oh, boy, that one went over big. Even Rebecca laughed. C'mon, Rebecca, let's get to the next one.

"The Sahara desert is located in . . . ?"

"Alabama," I yelled. I wasn't sure where it was located, but I knew it wasn't Alabama. I get a grunt of disgust from Rebecca, but a haw-haw from Cliff.

"A device mounted on the front of the train to help clear the track was called . . . ?" she asked.

"A firemen's hose," I shouted. That was pretty well received.

The next one: "Cotton is now picked by machine, but used to be picked by . . . ?"

"Lumberjacks" was the best I could do. It was getting stressful. I had to concentrate on pinochle too.

When Rebecca asked, "Arnold Palmer is a famous participant of what sport?" I hollered, "Girl watching."

My audience was tiring of me. Even the laughter from Cliff, my biggest fan, was dwindling. I sometimes wonder if a psychiatrist would classify this compulsion of mine as an obsessive-compulsive disorder—a real psychiatric problem. It certainly is a real social problem: It's called obnoxiousness.

Speaking of Cliff, we are an incongruous pair. I am large for a woman, and he is small for a man. He is eighty-seven years old but looks and acts much younger. His most prominent feature is his big smile.

We have a bond akin to that of husband and wife. When an older couple goes to bed for the night I picture them drinking a glass of warm milk, turning off the TV, turning off the lights, and going up to bed. Cliff and I have a nightly routine. We both go into the activities room after supper. Cliff is served a cup of coffee and cookies or cake or whatever. While he's drinking and eating, he often tells us a story about his younger, married days. (His wife is here too, but she's on life support and is non-functional.) Then he turns to me and says, "Well, good night, Jean."

I say, "Good night, Cliff."

He says, "Don't let the bed bugs bite."

I say, "If they do, I'll bite 'em right back."

Then he chuckles and wheels off to bed. I will miss this routine if Cliff dies before I do.

Cliff is one of our most contented residents. He participates in everything and seems to enjoy everything. I don't know whether his background has anything to do with it. I did his biography when I was writing the newspaper here, so I know a lot about him. His father died before he was born. His mother died when he was a year old—of a broken heart, his sister told him. Nobody in the family had enough money to take the responsibility of additional children, so Cliff and his siblings were sent to the German Roman Catholic orphanage on Pontiac Street. He says life was okay there. Cliff was appointed head of his table of fifteen to twenty kids, and everybody clamored to sit there because he was an expert at sneaking down to the kitchen and stealing extra portions of bread, milk, and butter. That the nuns never caught him is one of his greatest sources of pride.

When Cliff was in sixth grade, Catholic Charities placed him with a wealthy man and his wife who lived on suburban Main Street. Cliff worked in the garden and helped with the chickens, and—since the woman was an invalid—he had to help in the kitchen too. When the woman died, Catholic Charities placed Cliff on a farm in Westfield, where he was reunited with his brother who was one of seven boys living there. It was a commercial farm, and the work was hard, but the meals were good. In addition to the farm work he helped in the kitchen. But he balked at learning to milk the cows with the copout, "Oh, no, I'm a city boy."

Cliff became ill after a long potato-picking session in the rain without adequate outerwear. He was hospitalized and diagnosed as having arthritis in the legs. He was sent to a house on University Street to live with a blind woman who had raised his sister. While attending School 22 at Main and Oak Streets, he got a job cleaning a seamstress shop after school for fifty cents an hour. During the summers he also worked eight hours a day at the Orange Crush Bottling Company for thirty-five cents an hour.

At the age of sixteen he had to quit school to support himself. Through his uncle, he got a job (which turned out to be lifelong) at the Hewitt-Robbins Rubber Company. He met his future wife through a friend of his landlady.

His method of proposing was, "Will you provide a home for me, which I never had?"

"Sure, I will," Nina replied.

"She did a good job of it too," he said. In time they had a son, and the rest of his life story is normal. So what is it that makes him so contented now? His memories of a happy marriage? His feisty temperament that undoubtedly helped him survive his boyhood days? His genetic legacy? Sometimes I wonder if a temperament or disposition is dictated by endocrine balance more than outside influences. I'll bet even the neurologists and psychiatrists don't know the answer.

August 23

Adam died last night—cardiac arrest, I guess. (Don't we all die from cardiac arrest?) Adam was a successful businessman. He had an executive position with a fairly large corporation, and I assume it provided a living well above average for his wife and himself. I think he was once good looking—his eyes were still blue and his white hair was quite abundant—but he was much too heavy by the time he died. Three years ago he came here because his wife could no longer cope at home. He was in an advanced stage of Alzheimer's. He would escape whenever he could and then not be able to find his way home. After the police had to look for him a few times, his wife decided a protected environment was a necessity.

One day not too long ago he was agitated about something. I was about to use the phone in the lobby. Adam yanked it away from me so he could call the police. He dialed the operator (I found it interesting that he knew enough to dial the operator) and asked for the police, and the conversation was so funny I made a record of it:

"Hello, police? I'm being held here against my will in the beauty parlor. . . . I came over to do some business and they won't let me out. . . . I don't know where it is. . . . Well, there's an auto parts store across the street." This was not true, of course, but Adam continued to explain his imagined predicament to the person on the other end of the line. "I don't know what city I'm in." He turned and called to Peter, another resident, to tell the police what city he was in. "Ernie! Ernie! E-r-n-ie!" he called. But Ernie didn't answer because his name was Peter. "The background noise? Well, I don't know. There's people walking around and talking. . . . I don't know who they are. . . . 911? Okay."

He hung up and dialed 911 and went through the routine again.

The supervisor tried to take the phone and explain, but he wouldn't let her have it on the grounds that "You're one of them." Dolores eventually got it away from him by telling him she would explain it to 911, and he should wait on the bench for them. He went over to the bench immediately.

Alzheimer's residents are sometimes entertaining to the rest of us. Adam's wife died a year ago, and he has no children, so I think we can allow ourselves to be "entertained" when it doesn't hurt anyone.

Evan is another Alzheimer's resident who was an important man in his productive days. Evan is close to six feet tall, in his late seventies, slender, but with a paunch now. His white hair is sparse, but he has the vestiges of a ruggedly handsome face. He was a pilot during World War ll. He dropped parachutists into the Himalayas to rescue downed fliers. During the Korean War he flew a bomber. After the war he worked for Bell Laboratories, which sent him to Cape Canaveral to work with the first seven astronauts on the Mercury project.

He has been here for about five years, and we have watched him go through many stages of the disease. When he first came here he still knew his wife. Eventually he lost that orientation, and he claimed Agnes, another resident, as his wife. They often sat on the sofa in the lobby and cuddled like two lovers.

Sometimes he'd look for his car keys because, "I have to be in Montreal (or Toronto) tonight." Mr. C. or one of the staff would take him out to the parking lot to show him that his car was not there, or they would tell him it was in the repair shop. Sometimes he planned to take Agnes with him, and he would tell her she'd better get packed. Sometimes he'd forget by the time he got back to his room. If he hadn't forgotten, he'd become frustrated because he couldn't find his luggage. The staff would stall by telling him it was in storage in the basement, and they'd have to find the maintenance man who had the key.

Mr. C. would let Evan think that he was his assistant. Mr. C. would tell him as he left for the weekend, "Take care of things while I'm gone." This reinforced Evan's assumption that he was living a normal life. His disease has progressed now, and if he talks at all, he produces more guttural sounds than words. But I have noticed something very interesting. His body language tells me he still thinks he's in charge. He often sits with one leg crossed over the other, the top leg swinging slightly. The fingers of one hand drum the table while he surveys his surroundings like a supervisor making sure everything is going well. He certainly is not unhappy.

A couple of weeks ago I saw an article in the newspaper that proclaimed something like "Estrogen Found to Delay Onset of Alzheimer's Disease." Something interrupted me, and I didn't get a chance to read the whole article, but I found it pretty exciting that something may have been found to help the potential victims of this most ruthless of dignity destroyers.

13

The Merry Walkers

August 25, 1996

WE WHO LIVE IN THIS HOME have one big advantage over you guys out in the big world. We don't need a calendar to tell us what day of the week it is. The bananas tell us. They come in on Tuesdays after breakfast. On Wednesday morning they are yellow with a couple of brown flecks, on Thursday there's a few more brown flecks, on Friday several more, and on Saturday they're loaded with brown. On Sunday they're almost all brown and barely firm. On Monday they're solid brown and inedible. On Tuesday they're mush. Then the sequence starts over again.

August 27

Della is one of our happiest residents—and probably the most capricious. Her twinkly eyes attest to this. She is slim and has large features and sunken cheeks, which somehow make her attractive. She wears her brown, flecked-with-gray hair in curved bangs, which gives her a coquettish air. Whatever has happened in her brain, all it's done so far is to make her pleasantly confused. She's smiley and bouncy most of the time. All the staff agrees that she must have been a corker in her day, someone we'd all liked to have had in our social circles.

She travels around the building in a merry walker. That's a seat on wheels with a rail around it. Two straps come up between her thighs and fasten onto the front of the rail. She walks with her hands on the front of the rail. Anytime she gets tired, she plops and lands in the seat.

Della usually likes me and is conspiratorial *with* me, but today I was her target. Trixie was sitting on the arm of the chair next to me, and we were chatting for a few minutes after lunch. As I turned around to leave the dining room, Della was behind me, and I heard her say to Trixie, "She [referring to I don't know whom] just told me she was trying to steal him [referring to Evan] away from me."

I said to Trixie, "Is she talking about me?"

"M-m-m-huh," Trixie said with a barely suppressed giggle.

I said, "Della, I am not. I've got a husband. He'd kill me if I ever looked at another man."

Della ignored me as if I weren't there.

"She thinks she's Mrs. America," she said to Trixie, leaning forward to emphasize her words.

"I know she does," Trixie's replied.

Della went on, with her neck thrust forward again. "She eats like a pig."

"I know she does," Trixie agreed.

As Della turned to leave, she had a parting shot. "I saw them hugging and kissing. They ought to throw her in the river."

By now Trixie was giggling too hard to reply. But it didn't matter. Della was out of the dining room and on her way by then.

I was astounded, although I shouldn't have been because I've found the dementia patterns to be unpredictable. This was the first time Della had shown hostility to me. I'm usually her cohort, and we laugh together over her observations about someone else. Now I know what it's like to be on the other side of the fence.

I hope she remains this way. These are the residents who are the most fun.

August 28

We had our monthly residents' council meeting last week. At each meeting I read the minutes and then mention each department, asking if anyone has any concerns about that department. This is the time for residents to bring up any complaints and ask any questions. The complaints might be, "I didn't get my pink blouse back from the laundry yet," or "The spaghetti sauce wasn't hot enough last time," or "The spaghetti sauce was too hot last time," or "I asked them to put a lock on my closet door, and they haven't done it yet." The department heads are usually there to answer complaints.

I went through the departments one by one asking for comments. When I asked about the maintenance department, Lou, one of our newest tenants, said, "Conscientious, they do good work." When I got to social services, Lou said, "Excellent." When I got to physical therapy, he said the same thing.

Well, I thought to myself, I've got to find out the circumstances of his being here. His elevator still went all the way to the top, so I knew his comments were sincere. How could a man who had both legs amputated and had to go to a nursing home have such a positive outlook?

August 29

It was nearing one o'clock yesterday, and I was almost to the dining room door when a middle-aged woman, whom I'd never seen before, stopped me.

"Are you Jean?" she asked.

"Yes," I admitted.

"I'm a friend of Grace's," she said. "I know you are a friend of hers, so I thought I'd visit her and you too. I brought you each a little gift." She pulled a gift-wrapped package out of her bag. "Are you going to eat now? How long will it take you?"

"Usually about half an hour, but I'll try to hurry."

"Oh, no," she said. "Take your time. I won't be able to wait. My husband's in the car."

"Bring him in," I invited.

"Oh, he won't come in. He's afraid of nursing homes. I'll call you next week."

I didn't have to respond because she was off to find Grace. But here it was again—the nursing home paranoia syndrome. For those who feel that way, I have to resort to a cliché again. *If you haven't tried it, don't knock it.*

Doug once told me, "There are a whole bunch of people out there who think we're in here beating you people up."

I had responded scoffingly, "Aw, c'mon, you're kidding."

"No, I'm not."

I guess maybe he wasn't.

Grace is another painful subject. She was a close neighbor and one of my closest friends. She was an attractive woman with a lovely disposition—kind, gentle, a true lady. She's no longer attractive. When the mind goes, it shows in the face immediately. Between twenty-five and thirty years ago, her only sister and her only brother died. Then her only child was in an auto accident that caused internal injuries severe enough to make his survival doubtful for about two weeks. (He did survive and is fine now.) All this happened within a two-year period. She had a nervous breakdown—a catchall term. She did the sensible thing—she saw a psychiatrist. The psychiatric sessions were fine, but he also put her on medication. The last time I saw her, right before I came here, her lips were thick and her speech was slurred.

I said, "Grace, have you considered reducing the medication?"

"No," she said, "he didn't say I should." She said it as if she were drunk, but I knew she didn't drink. Both her niece and I think overmedication contributed, if only in a small way, to her being here.

Grace's husband died around 1984. Her son and daughter-in-law added two rooms onto their house and brought her to live with them. That worked out fine for several years, but Grace is a tall woman (about five foot eleven), and her daughter-in-law is less than five feet. Eventually her daughter-in-law could no longer handle her physically, so in June of 1991, Grace became my neighbor once again. She no longer knew me by then, so it wasn't a happy reunion. She went through years here of intermittent anxiety until the right balance of medication was found. She still has periods of lunacy (I don't know what other word to use) when she goes "Ga . . . ga . . . ga . . . ga . . . ga . . . ga . . . ga," but they're shorter and less frequent.

August 31

I talked to Lou today about his positive attitude. I asked him the circumstances of his being here. He said diabetes robbed him of his legs. He's a slightly built man with pleasant features, and he looks more like sixty-four than his actual age of seventy-four years. After he had the first leg amputated, about a year and a half ago, he was still able to hop around on the other with the help of a walker. But after he had the second one amputated, he could no longer use the walker, so a nursing home was the only answer. He told me he has had seventeen operations, which include two heart bypasses and six operations on one knee alone.

I mentioned that so many people enter a nursing home with resistance, and they spend a lot of time moaning, "I want to go home."

Lou said, "Sure, I'd like to go home too, but I know I can't."

When I asked about his positive attitude, he said he prays every night for the courage to handle whatever comes with a positive outlook.

God must have answered his prayers.

"And," he added, "I guess St. Peter isn't ready for me yet."

September 3

I wheeled up to my room to be put to bed after Rudy, Mildred, and I finished our almost-nightly hour and a quarter of pinochle. The aide whose slot I was assigned to asked, "Did you hear what happened to . . . Oh, maybe I shouldn't say anything."

"What? What?"

"Oh, I don't think I should have said anything."

"What?" At this point, my sole purpose in life became to find out what she thought she shouldn't have told me. "C'mon," I urged.

"Well . . ." She hesitated. "Edith died a little while ago."

I think the aides feel that hearing about the death of someone will upset us. "Oh, that's wonderful," I said.

My reaction puzzled her, just as I am puzzled by the aides' responses to the release of these old people who have been suffering for months. No matter how old and sick the person is, the aides, being young, think death is the worst thing that could happen. Edith was my former beautician, the giver whose home was open to any and all who needed it. If you remember, a brain tumor had been slowly draining the life from her, and now it was accomplished. I'm happy for her and her whole family.

September 4

My sister called last night. We're really cousins, but my mother died when I was six years old, and her mother and father raised me. Her father was my father's brother. She's only eight months older than me, and we've always considered ourselves sisters.

She was full of news. A dear friend from our younger days had died, a dear friend of hers had just been sent home from the hospital to die of non-Hodgkin's lymphoma, and worst of all, our Pennsylvania cousin's twenty-two-year-old grandson had been killed. He was in the army, stationed in Kentucky. When his unit returned from maneuvers, they found that one of the men was missing a hand grenade. The bomb squad was sent out to look for it. They couldn't find it. The men themselves were sent back to look for it. One of them stepped on it. He was killed instantly, another soldier lost a leg, and my cousin's grandson got shrapnel in the neck and heart.

No one who hasn't been through it can imagine the horror of losing a child. I suspect that to lose one through an accident is worse than through an illness, where you have some notice of what's ahead. Fortunately, my Pennsylvania cousin died several months ago, the eventual result of a stroke, so at least she was spared this grief.

September 5

I was excited. I told Laura (south wing coordinator) about an article I had just read in *The Readers Digest* about Redux, the latest diet pill. It suppresses a brain signal that triggers hunger. When the serotonin level in the brain is high, your hunger is abated. Redux keeps the serotonin level high. The article mentioned that an "exceedingly rare, but potentially life-threatening side effect has been documented: primary pulmonary hypertension (PPH)." It happened in eighteen out of a million people. Not bad odds—unless you were one of the eighteen. I told Laura I was going to ask the doctor for a prescription.

September 6

Laura came in first thing in the morning and said she heard an alert on the news about Redux. It was apt to cause PPH—just what the article said—but according to the news bulletin, it wasn't all that rare. She said she wouldn't have paid any attention to the report if I hadn't mentioned Redux the day before. Back to square one.

September 6 evening

Our card group pulled up to the table for our usual afternoon session. Mildred had great difficulty. I've mentioned that she's paralyzed on the left side. She has a board with a slot in it in which to put her cards. Today she could hardly get the cards in. They kept going onto the floor and the table. Her fingers wouldn't do what she wanted them to do. At first I thought it was funny—that she was having a clumsy day. Then I realized she had lost fine motor control. A small stroke? The beginning of a stroke?

In the evening she was better but not normal. I told the nurse. She said she'd make a note of it for Laura.

September 7

Mildred wasn't as bad today, but she's still not normal.

September 8

Mildred couldn't play cards today. Her good arm is numb now.

September 9

Mildred went to the hospital at four fifteen this afternoon. She was incoherent.

September 13 (Friday)

Our luncheon group had lunch at the nearby Chinese restaurant. It was raining as it had been for days. I wore a throwaway poncho that Trixie gave me and a towel over my legs. I couldn't hold the umbrella so that it covered Rudy (the Liz Claiborne is really mine, I guess), so he just got wet. There were nine of us. Whitney, the former weekend receptionist, was there. I haven't seen her since last December. She was supposed to have been at Margaret's retirement party. She paid for her ticket, but she never showed up. Now I know why. She thought it was the following night.

In the afternoon, Mildred came home from the hospital. She's paralyzed on both sides now, but her speech is intact again.

September 15

It rained hard all night. I lay in bed thinking how cozy it was to be warm and dry when the elements were strutting their stuff. This morning the aides were talking about the street in front of the nursing home. Tracey said the water was up to her waist. Yvette said it floated her car like a boat. Al, our head of maintenance, usually isn't here on weekends, but he had to come in. Our basement flooded.

Tracey came into my room this morning about ten thirty and said Mildred moved her foot. I hope it turns out to be as good as it sounds.

September 16

Mildred moved her arm up to her cheek in physical therapy and in occupational therapy.

September 23

Bernadette is the daytime weekend receptionist. We call her Bern. She's in the young middle-age category. She wears her dark hair in a short, modified pageboy similar to a 1920s bob. She has a beautiful complexion and is pleasant to look at, but she has one big flaw. Her fanny is approaching the dimensions of mine.

We usually exchange bits of gossip and the latest jokes. When some of the visitors we know well enter the lobby to leave the building, we share the jokes with them. Yesterday she said, "I wonder if the nursing home knows how we entertain the guests. They always leave laughing."

She once said, "Friends have said to me, 'How can you stand working in a nursing home?' They can't imagine what fun we have."

14

Bye, Bye, Blackbird

September 24, 1996

YOU'LL FIND A LOT OF PEOPLE with hearing disabilities in a nursing home. Sometimes the conversations remind me of a favorite old joke:

Three elderly British gentlemen were driving down the road in an English countryside. When they came to a village, the first man asked, "Is this Wembley?"

"No," said the second man, "it's Thursday."

"Me too," said the third, "let's stop and have a drink."

I was lucky enough to get in on a similar exchange yesterday morning. It was early in the morning. Some of the residents were in the hallway outside my room waiting to be wheeled to the dining room.

Madeleine, one of my fellow residents, started shouting, "I have to go to the toilet." Then louder, "Toilet!" And again at the top of her lungs, "Toilet! I want to shit. Where do I go to shit?"

Bessie, shouting in order to be heard over the din, said, "I want my sweater."

Madeleine responded, "You want to shit in your sweater?"

"Yeah, it might get chilly," Bessie said.

This same Madeleine was sitting behind me in the activities room one evening when I heard her say, "Why, you son of a bitch!"

She was behind me facing Eddie, in an old-fashioned love-seat position.

I wheeled around so I could see her. "Madeleine, what's the matter?"

"He said he'd buy me for ninety cents." She was indignant.

I tried to explain. "He doesn't know what he's saying."

In the meantime, Eddie continued saying, "Mumble, mumble, mumble."

"Ya can't talk to me like that, ya dirty old thing," Madeleine answered.

I can't imagine what Eddie had said, but I'm sure it wasn't what Madeleine heard. Sometimes the entertainment here is as good as a movie.

September 25

I had just about finished supper, and the aides, nurses, and I were shooting the bull in the dining room. I don't like to leave the table right after I eat. I like to sit and relax a while. There's time for me to do that because some of the residents are slow eaters, and I'm a fast eater. Somehow the talk turned to people not paying back money. The staff are not supposed to ask the residents if they can borrow money, but they ignore the rule when it comes to me, and I allow it.

"Yeah," I said, "that SOB Ted left here owing me seventeen dollars."

"What?" somebody said. "You jerk."

"Why did you give it to him?" somebody else said.

"Well, he had borrowed from me before—not much, just a few dollars—but he always paid me back," I said defensively. "This time, though, I was really a jerk. He said he needed $16.75 to get his car out of the garage so he wouldn't have to ride his bicycle to work. Rudy had just given me some spending money, so I had felt here was this man with a problem, and I was in a position to solve it, and it would be wrong of me not to."

"A $16.75 bill from an auto mechanic," somebody hooted. "What did he do, put air in his tires?" This brought a round of laughter from everybody, including me.

"So the next day his car caught fire," I told them. "I guess that was in case I noticed he was still riding his bicycle."

Some more snickers from my audience.

"Then he couldn't pay me the following week because he had more troubles than my roses had aphids. He said he would pay me half the week after and the other half the week after that."

I heard "Yeah, yeah, yeah" from my listeners. They'd been there.

"I said okay. Like I had a choice."

The laughter was too loud for me to add that he called in sick the next day, then stopped in to pick up his paycheck. I never saw him again.

Phyllis, the supervisor, said that's why she doesn't bring money to work anymore. About a year ago one of the aides left suddenly, owing her thirty dollars.

Well, I figure you only owe me twelve dollars, Ted. We had five dollars worth of fun tonight.

September 26

We have a lot of music here. We have a record player and a CD player and a player piano. The piano is quite new and has discs rather than the old fashioned rolls. We have some good discs for it. We have some good CDs too. We have some great records, but we also have some Mitch Miller records.

Now these are the songs that people sing at a party when everybody's in a good mood and they gather around a piano to liven things up: "Let Me Call You Sweetheart," "Beer Barrel Polka," "Bye, Bye, Blackbird," ad infinitum. That's fun when it's every five years or more, but when it's x number of times a week, the Golden Oldies become the Brass Moldies. (Of course, I'm being unfair. I still have my marbles. Those who have any of the dementias probably don't remember that they heard something twice this week already.) Not to mention that Fred's morning announcements sometimes include these same songs too.

A couple of days ago, I called Rebecca over and offered her five dollars if she would hide the Mitch Miller records in my closet for six months. (I could have done it myself, but I like to do my underhanded work honorably.)

She laughed appreciatively and said, "I can't take your money."

She thought for a moment, then said, "But I'll tell you what I'll do." She interrupted herself and got four records. "I'll put these four in your closet for two months. They include the biggest offender, 'Bye, Bye, Blackbird.'"

"Good enough," I said. I figured a two-month reprieve would be enough to build up my coping defenses again.

September 27

I solved my printer problem by buying a new one. But I had to get a new computer too. The printer I wanted was too sophisticated for my computer.

I'll probably have to update myself, too. This printer may not understand "Oh, shit" and "Oh, damn."

This evening, Rudy and I were playing two-handed pinochle in the dining room. There was a group in the activities room. Suddenly Angeline's daughter Toni burst into a robust laughter that broke my concentration. I wanted to know what was funny.

"Olivia said she was wet," explained Toni. Olivia is one of our more unhappily confused residents and has a heavy Polish accent. "Carla [an evening activities aide] asked how that happened, and Olivia said, 'Somebody took my pants off me, wet them, and put them back on me.' I said, 'That's unbelievable!' and she said, 'It is unbelievable, but it's true.'"

Olivia is not a happy camper. Sometimes she is, but most of the time she's looking for her daughter. She'll ask everyone who comes near her, "Have you seen Donna Wagner?"

Her daughter visits at regular intervals, but Olivia forgets as soon as she's gone. Sometimes it's her mother she's looking for.

I find it interesting that many of our residents are looking for their mothers, or are upset because their mothers are sick, or they want to call home to let their mothers know where they are so they won't worry.

It reminds me of the true story of the seventy-six-year-old man who was ready to be discharged from the hospital. He was asked how he was getting home.

"My mother's picking me up," he said.

It was decided they'd better keep him another day and do a psychiatric evaluation. This evaluation turned out fine, so they told him again he could go home, and then they waited to see what would happen. He made a phone call, and a half hour later his ninety-six-year-old mother and her ninety-seven-year-old sister drove over and picked him up.

September 28

Some of the staff have been after me to get the football squares started, so I did yesterday. If any of you don't know what football squares are, I will explain: We draw one hundred squares on a sheet of paper, ten one-inch or larger squares across and down. Those who want to participate buy a square for two dollars. When all the squares are sold, we assign numbers randomly across the top and down one side.

We accomplish the randomness by shuffling the ace through ten from a deck of playing cards, then writing in the numbers first across the top, then down one side as the numbers are turned over one by one. The ten stands for zero. We write the name of one team across the top. We write the name of the team they're playing down the side. It doesn't matter who wins or loses; it's only the score that counts.

The person whose name is in the square where the last numbers of each score intersect at the end of each quarter wins the money. For example, if the Jets have seven and the Dolphins have fourteen at the end of the first quarter, you run your finger across the top until you get to the seven, then run your finger down that column until you come to the four. The person whose name is in that square wins thirty-five dollars.

We pay after each quarter—thirty-five, forty, and forty-five dollars, and then fifty dollars for the final score. The residents' council keeps thirty dollars for sponsoring it. It adds zip to watching the games.

Today we didn't need any extra zip. When I wheeled into the dining room for supper, Ethel was doing her non-stop monologuing, Grace was hollering, "Mother! Mother! Mother!" and Gretchen was shrieking at her neighbor over ownership of space at the long dinner table. As if that weren't enough zip for one night, Velma bellowed the first verse of "The Star Spangled Banner" over all the noise. It was a cacophony that would have made Bellevue envious.

September 30

Elise (the one with the gorgeous white hair) and I sit together at the dining table nearest the door. If I let the legs of my wheelchair down, there's room for one more person. Today Paula, head of dietary, asked if I minded if Norma sat with us. Norma usually eats in her room out of preference, but they were trying to encourage her to eat more, and Paula thought that having pleasant company might help.

I could never figure out if Norma had all her marbles or not. Sometimes she seemed to, and sometimes not quite. We were halfway through lunch, and Norma was dawdling, still not very enthusiastic about eating.

Trying to be helpful, I said, "Eat your fish, Norma. Then you can have dessert."

"Will you push it down for me?" she responded.

"I can't. I'm in a wheelchair."

Norma (who's also in a wheelchair) said, "That's too bad."

My sarcastic nature asserted itself. "Yeah. Life is rough."

"Why?" asked Norma. "Do you sit on sandpaper?"

I don't have to worry about her marbles. She's got more than I have.

Kate, our social worker, hates the phrase, "All her marbles." She's concerned about dignity, which is her job. If I start to use it, a look from her stops me before I get any further than, "Has she got—"

Kate is another petite. She is a tailored person, fond of wearing suits. Her hair is short and straight, reminiscent of the old Dutch Boy Paint advertisements. If she's not bent on a serious errand, her even features have the look of someone who is about to perform or who has just performed a bit of mischief. Kate spent seven years as a nun many years ago. Kate's sense of humor in a convent? It boggles the mind.

Maybe the nuns have hearing disabilities too.

15

Each New Deal

October 3, 1996

RUDY AND I WENT to Winona Heights Retirement Home for lunch yesterday. Some of the retirement homes put invitations in the senior citizen newspapers inviting anyone who is interested to come for lunch. They give you lunch and then show you through the facility, trying to attract tenants. The lunch was delicious, but I felt the rooms were too stark. They could have used some warm colors on the walls and perhaps in the window treatments. We went to Apple Tree Lane Retirement Home two weeks ago under the same conditions.

If you have the privilege of choosing, the look and atmosphere of a nursing home makes a difference. Everyone wants to feel at home rather than like they're living in an institution. But I have found that the quality of the people you have to live with matters more. Maybe these places should instead line up their staff and invite potential residents to come in and interview them, hassle them, and tell corny jokes. When you find lots of hard-working treasures who know what it means to overcome adversity and still laugh at themselves, that's where you'll want to be. I guess I got lucky that way.

I got lucky another way, too. I forgot to tell you that on July 1, a wheelchair van service, offered by our bus transit system and subsidized by the government, went into effect in our suburb. It's a door-to-door pickup and delivery service for the disabled. It costs five dollars for a round trip for the disabled person and nothing for the attendant. There are four zones. Each additional zone entered is one dollar extra for a round trip. It's a wonderful service.

Rudy wants to go to our favorite seafood restaurant next week. So do I, but oh boy! It is a cholesterol lover's paradise.

October 7

The winners of the football pool were Kate, Cindy (head of housekeeping), Doug, and Barbara, the north wing aide who bought the large chocolate penis for a centerpiece. None of them bought as many squares as I did, but if you're hot you're hot, and if you're not you're not. Speaking of Barbara, she is the luckiest person at winning money I've ever known. Her latest coup occurred last week: a seven-hundred-dollar win on the Lucky 7 Lotto.

October 8

Mildred went back to the hospital. Things don't look as good as they did at first. She could be in for a long hard fight.

October 10

I had just pulled up to the supper table when Jenny (the south wing aide who makes two syllables out of *shit*) came over and said, "Wanna see something?"

Of course I did. She pulled a Lucky 7 Lotto ticket out of her pocket. There it was—three sevens in a row, and under "Prize" was printed "700." Damn! I never get more than forty dollars.

October 11

We had our weekly poker session last night. Rudy was the only winner. Doug organized the poker game about two months ago when he found out Lou (one of our most upbeat residents) liked to play. My usual luck seems to have left me. The nice thing about card games is that no matter how bad things are going, each new deal is a new beginning. If we viewed life that way, and substituted day for deal, there'd be more optimism around.

Maybe.

I was just finishing supper when one of the aides said, "You have company, two women and a man."

I wheeled out to the lobby, and there was my former next-door neighbor's son, and his wife and daughter. My delight in seeing them was short-lived. They had come to tell me his mother had died two weeks before. They had brought her ashes up to be buried in the family plot.

My neighbor Anne and her family moved to Miami thirty years ago. We always remained in touch. But since I hadn't seen her in thirty years, my reaction at the news of her death surprised me. I felt abandoned. *How could you leave me like that, Anne?*

October 12

It's Saturday night, and Rosalia's on duty in activities. The regular aide had some function at church so Wanda, the activities director, called Rosalia and said she'd have to cover. Rosalia had planned a birthday party for her son with twenty-three guests invited. She had to switch it to the afternoon. I hope Wanda appreciates Rosalia.

October 15

Terry called. Robin's no better and no worse. The doctor thinks the new MS medication may have put her into remission. It almost seems cruel to put her into remission at the stage she's in. It angers me, perhaps unjustifiably. But with all the publicity about new medications to help MS, how come nothing has helped Robin?

October 19

It is cold today. Two days ago Rudy and I had a picnic lunch in the backyard here. Now you can feel winter in the air.

October 20

I think Somebody Up There is out to get me. Our tape deck is back. It was out to be repaired. Now we are playing our tapes again. So we're back to "Bye, Bye, Blackbird." Philosophically speaking, I guess a few weeks reprieve is better than nothing.

October 21

I distributed the money to the winners of our second football pool. Cindy won again. She is so lucky at this stuff. Some of the staff are threatening that they won't participate if I sell any more tickets to her. I hope they're kidding because I won't bar anybody from participating. There are a lot of football fans here.

On the Sundays our team plays, the staff is allowed to wear Buffalo Bills sweatshirts, and most of them do. Some of the residents do too. Excitement runs high. When we make a touchdown, there's a lot of hooting. If we lose, there's a lot of

Monday morning quarterbacking—what who should have done when. I'll bet our team doesn't know how supportive we are.

October 22

That Jenny! She's too much. Last night after I got in bed, I wanted popcorn. I gave her seventy cents to go down in the basement and get a package out of the vending machine. She came back up and said there were two packages of cupcakes in front of the popcorn. I wasn't about to buy two packages of cupcakes in order to get some popcorn, so *I* said, "Oh, she-it," and went back to my reading.

I fell asleep sitting up with the book on my chest. In a while I felt somebody shaking my arm. Jenny was standing there with a bagful of microwave-popped corn. She had gotten in her car during her break time, driven three blocks down the street, bought the popcorn, then came back and microwaved it. They say you shouldn't spoil children. Well, she spoils me, and all its done is make me love her. What's so bad about that?

Mildred came home from the hospital this afternoon. I met her daughter in the hallway in the evening. In answer to my question Leslie said her mother wasn't doing well at all.

"She's very confused," Leslie said.

That's how Mildred seemed to me too. She didn't seem to know who I was when I tried to talk to her.

October 23

I suppose there are a few ways to spoil children. Or maybe they spoil themselves.

Virginia is the night supervisor. Her sixteen-year-old daughter answered an ad in the paper looking for someone interested in housing a foreign exchange student. The upshot was that, at the end of August, Virginia welcomed into her family an eighteen-year-old Russian girl named Yma. Virginia brought her in one day and I met her. She's a tall, slender brunette, very pretty. She looks as if she's very careful of her diet.

Well, I guess she is, but not in the orthodox way. She's doing it in the bulimic way. Virginia says she's eating them out of house and home and then throwing it up. Yma denies it, but Virginia hears her, despite her attempts to hide it by running the water. Virginia says her eating pattern supports the bulimia theory too. If they're at a restaurant or someone's house, where it's not convenient to throw up, Yma eats very little. Virginia spoke to the area representative. She feels the girl's mother should know. Or maybe she does know?

Lou played poker yesterday with Doug, Rudy, Al (head of maintenance), and Al's friend. Boy, did Lou kick butt.

October 24

Damn! I went to get the picture frame I bought last week, and it wasn't there. Yes, that is one of the bad things about nursing homes. Property does get stolen.

I recently saw a cute Irish blessing in a catalog. It was framed and cost twenty dollars, probably twenty-five with postage and handling. So I figured I could buy cheap frames, print a bunch of the blessings myself, and give them to my kids in their Christmas boxes and to a few other people.

The same thing happened with a new, three-ring, loose-leaf notebook. Gosh, how I envy the moral standards of the people who can pick up whatever they want. If my aunt and uncle who raised me hadn't forbidden me to do that sort of thing, I might have a diamond and emerald ring by now. But most of the aides are honest. It's a very small minority that we run into now and then that do the dirty work.

On behalf of that small minority, I now share with you the Irish blessing:

> *May those who love us, love us.*
> *And those that don't love us,*
> *May God turn their hearts.*
> *And if He doesn't turn their hearts,*
> *May He turn their ankles*
> *So we'll know them by their limping.*
> *—Anonymous*

October 26

An aide wheeled Mildred past me when she was going back to her room. How sad it is to see her this way. She loved playing cards so much. It's very possible she doesn't even remember now that she used to play.

October 27

We set the clocks back last night. That is, everybody did except one of the north wing aides. He forgot. When this happens, it's a tossup about which is worse—the ribbing you have to take from the night shift or the sacrifice of that extra hour you could have spent in bed.

October 30

The Halloween party this year was chaos. Two years ago Wanda instituted a Halloween party for the staff, their children, and the residents. Last year and the year before, it was great. Word must have gotten around that it was great. This year it was mobbed. The kids had to take turns by age playing the games.

There were prizes for the kids, and doughnuts and cider for everybody. It was fun watching them play musical chairs and eating doughnuts tied to a broomstick with their hands tied behind their backs. We'll have to talk about what to do next year. It's been suggested that we have it just for the kids. The parents can leave. We'll see.

November 5

My sister came over to visit. She didn't bring any pistachio nuts, thank goodness! She knows I love them and that it's a temptation I can't resist, so she's trying to be cooperative.

November 8

Rudy and I went out for lunch yesterday to a restaurant we've never been to before. We took the Paratransit service for the disabled. The weather was gorgeous. I didn't even wear a sweater.

It's the same today.

November 9

I woke up to a blanket of snow. Yesterday and the day before were like spring. Now this.

November 11

The winners of the football pool were Barbara (first and second quarters), Lou, and Toni. Incredible! Barbara is lucky at everything. Barbara and Lou won last time too. This is the first time for Toni, but she wins every time we play poker.

November 16

We had a baked goods sale yesterday. I'm so ashamed, I won't tell you how much I bought. I use the rationale that I'm going to eat it for breakfast, and that the breakfast calories don't count as long as I stick to my low-calorie cereal for supper. Anyway, I gave most of it to Rudy.

One of the housekeeping aides baked two coffee cakes that could have been entered in a contest. They had the usual walnuts and raisins, but what made them unusual was that the cinnamon was throughout the cake instead of being confined to streaks. This gave it the color of a pale chocolate cake. Icing was dribbled on. It was the best I've ever had. She should be working in her own bakery.

We made $129. Not bad.

November 27

I did it again—got screwed on a loan. It's no big deal, only three dollars, but I am such a jerk. The signs were all there, and I ignored them. About five days ago an aide was chatting while she was getting me dressed.

"My father isn't speaking to me," she said.

"Why not?" I responded.

"I bought four thousand dollars worth of furniture, and he cosigned the loan. I haven't made any payments yet. He's had to make them all."

I just shook my head, but I was thinking, what business does a girl in your economic situation have buying four thousand dollars worth of furniture on credit?

That afternoon I wheeled out to the lobby about one o'clock, and the aide was standing there with her coat on. It was too early for her shift to end. I heard somebody ask her what she was doing.

"Waiting for my ride," she replied.

She leaned over and whispered in my ear, "Can I borrow three dollars for gas?"

It turned out that she had been fired, which was why she was going home early. The next day I asked the receptionist to tell her to see me when she picked up her check a few days later. She did see me. Rudy and I were playing cards with Herb and Sophia. The aide came over and whispered, "I'll get my check cashed and be right back with your money." I never saw her again.

The signs were there: four thousand dollars worth of furniture and sticking your father with the payments? Leaving at one o'clock? That would mean you were sick or fired. She didn't look sick. Somebody's picking you up, but you need money for gas? See what I mean by ignoring the signs? That's why I feel like a jerk.

It's a good thing I've got administrators who can handle the firing of people like that. My gullibility scares me sometimes. It's the same thing when baked goods tell me they won't make me fat. Apparently I need someone to fire all the muffins and coffee cakes too.

December 2

Rudy made dinner for Thanksgiving and brought it over here—seafood salad and broccoli-cheese puffs. Rosalia's sister baked us a pumpkin pie. 'Twas a meal fit for a king—a belly-over-his-belt kind of king. I loved it. The day after, Rudy flew to Florida to spend a week with the kids.

About a week ago, Ronnie (the night shift aide who makes such fun of my fanny) came into my room at eleven thirty and said, "Do you remember Andrea who used to work here—heavy girl, thick lips, very vibrant?"

I did remember her because she was so outrageously funny. She was the one who bought her own Valentine's Day candy to make her boyfriend jealous. She used to say that when her mother came over to her house and she didn't answer the door because she didn't feel like talking to anybody, her mother would pound on the door and say, "Open up yo hussy. I know yo in there." She said it loud and with gestures, and she kept us laughing.

Ronnie said, "I just heard on the news that she was arrested on several counts of resident abuse [at another nursing home]."

I was stunned. She didn't seem like that type. What's "that type," right? It made me feel depressed for a while.

We're making plans to go to Angelo's Italian Manor again on December 23.

16

Not Enough to Worry About

December 9, 1996

DOLORES, THE AIDE WHO LOST the six million dollar lottery, came to work this afternoon with a dilly of a tale. She and Hank, her husband, went to a wedding reception for Hank's cousin's son at the Fireside Inn last Saturday. They didn't know that the Fireside has three rooms for receptions, so they walked into the first one they came to. Not having seen the groom in years and never having seen the bride, they expected them to be strangers. They kissed the bride, congratulated the groom, and handed him a card with a hefty bill in it. When they started to circulate and saw no familiar faces, suspicion crept in. They investigated and found the reception they wanted was in the next room. Now the problem was to retrieve the card with the hefty bill in it.

"C'mon," said Hank, "we have to go back."

"I don't have to go," Dolores said. "You can get it by yourself."

"I don't want to go alone," he pleaded. "I don't know what to say."

"It's your relative that's getting married," said Dolores. "Just tell the guy the truth."

"It would be easier if you were with me."

Dolores had already made her peace with losing the money. She had already lost the lottery—how much could a little more hurt? She wasn't going back in that room for anything. But she decided that if she could con Hank into doing the dirty work, then the victory would be all the better. So she scoffed at her husband's displeasure. "Listen, Hank," she said, "it's no big deal. I'll be right here."

After dragging his feet for several minutes, all the while being encouraged by Dolores, Hank went back and retrieved the card.

"See," Dolores said, "it wasn't so bad, was it?" One look at his face and she could hardly keep the laughter from erupting.

I think I would have wheeled out of that room and kept on going. *Sayōnara*, hefty bill. It was nice knowing ya.

December 10

We had our annual bazaar on Friday and Saturday. It's always pretty good, but as I've said, relatives who are visiting people in their rooms don't come back to where the bazaar is. They don't pay attention to signs, so it's mostly staff that are the customers. Next year maybe we can have displays on a couple of card tables in the atrium, where the entrance is, to attract people's attention. Then we can tell them where the main event is.

Penny's mother always has a table full of beautiful items to sell, but she didn't have as many this year because her attention was needed elsewhere. She made us a gold satin angel to raffle. I haven't had a chance to sell raffle tickets yet because of getting boxes ready to be sent out of state to my family. The guilt is beginning to overtake me. I'll have to get busy on it.

December 14

THE STATE came on December 9 this year, almost a month earlier than the last few years. They probably wanted to take us by surprise. Well, they did. There's one little problem we have to correct. We have a couple of cases of decubitus (bed sores), but we had them pretty well under control already.

January 2, 1997

We had a hot-ding party on New Year's Eve. We turned the clock ahead four and a half hours and used seven thirty as our midnight. Rosalia, Trixie, and one of our volunteers were in charge. They gave the countdown at 7:29:50 and we toasted the New Year with champagne. Then we ate Chex mix, egg rolls, and pizza roll, along with cheese, baloney and ham on Triscuits. We whoop-de-dooed till eight fifteen, then drifted off to bed.

January 10

I've been to the computer only once in weeks. So many piddlin' little things to take care of. Twelve of us went to Angelo's for lunch on the twenty-third. Our daughter Peggy came in from Texas on the evening of the twenty-fourth and stayed for five days. We ate out twice and went to the mall by utilizing the bus service for the disabled. We stayed up every night until midnight or one thirty playing cards. It was a hectic pace. Nice to find out I was able to tolerate it.

January 11

Terry stopped in to see me. Robin is the same. It's always fun gossiping with Terry. We exchange little happenings in our lives. I started to tell Terry what happened to me at Angelo's when we went there at Christmastime.

"Oh, him," she said, interrupting me. "I would never go there again." This sounded good, but she told me to tell my story first.

"Well, twelve of us went there for lunch on December 23," I said. "We had a delicious meal—at least I did. I had some sort of steak with béarnaise sauce, which was excellent, and so was the Caesar salad.

"I had gotten there by the wheelchair van service, and I ordered a two thirty pickup, which meant I had to be ready by two fifteen because the rules state you have to allow for the bus to be fifteen minutes early or fifteen minutes late. Our waiter started passing out our checks at about ten after two. Then he picked them up again, saying there was a mistake. He took them wherever and was gone for a long time.

"Rudy was getting antsy because of the bus schedule. With Rudy antsy means, 'Where the hell are they, those assholes. Doesn't anybody around here know what they're doing?' and so on."

I leaned conspiratorially toward Terry, reliving the story even as I continued telling it. "Rosalia said under her breath, 'Are you mortified?'

"I answered her, 'Yes,' also under my breath. About twenty-five after two, our waiter came back with the corrected bills. We made our way to the lobby. Rudy got in the cashier's line while I checked to see if the bus was there. It wasn't, so he relaxed a bit.

"That night when Rosalia got here for activities aide duty, we rehashed our afternoon.

"'You know,' she told me, 'there was a check left on our table, so I picked it up then didn't know what to do with it. It was for $15.01. Harry said, "Put it down there," indicating a table in the lobby. I heard somebody say, "I think it belongs to the lady in the wheelchair.""""

Terry gasped. "Oh no," she said.

I took it that my storytelling was communicating the gist of my humiliation and continued with my dramatic rendition, which was every bit the truth. "So I looked at Rosalia stupidly. 'My God! Do you think Rudy was so mad that he didn't pay his bill?' That was the amount of his bill. Mine was more. I told her that I'd have to call Angelo in the morning.

"I didn't get the chance. I was barely up and dressed before he called me.

"'Hello, Jean. This is Angelo,' he began. 'We threw your credit card number away.'

"I had to give my credit card number when I made the reservation," I explained to Terry. "Then if we had been no-calls-no-shows, I would have been charged twenty-five dollars."

"Did you give him your number again?" Terry asked.

"No," I said. "I told him, 'I know what you're calling about, Angelo. Rosalia told me about the leftover check last night. Let me talk to my husband, and I'll call you back this afternoon.'

"Rudy and I had lunch together, and I asked him, 'Did you pay for your lunch yesterday?'

"He looked at me puzzled and said, 'Why, of course, I paid.'

"I knew immediately that he had," I told Terry. "If he hadn't, he would have said something like, 'You're goddam right I didn't, and I don't intend to. Those assholes didn't know what the hell they were doing. If everybody ran a restaurant that way there wouldn't be any place to eat out. They'd better learn.' Everybody I've told who knows him agrees with me on this."

Terry shook her head in agreement.

"I told him about Angelo's call. Rudy said he gave the cashier thirty-five dollars, and she gave him a dollar and some cents in change. So I called Angelo back and said, 'Rudy said he did pay, and I know he's telling the truth.'

"Angelo said there was an unpaid bill that appeared to be his. I said it must have been a duplication. He said the computer didn't show a duplication. All I could do was insist that Rudy paid.

"He said, 'All right, we'll let it go.' I could tell by his inflection that he didn't believe me.

"Every time I tried to tell somebody about it, I would start crying because I knew he didn't believe me. Even three days later I woke up crying.

"That morning Val called me and said, 'I spoke to Angelo this morning. I knew you were upset so I called him. Rudy was ahead of me in line, and I knew he paid two checks, so I told him that.'

"'What did he say?' I asked.

"She said, 'He told me they had so much business this year that they had to hire waiters from other restaurants, and they had a lot of problems. But they learned a lot, and next year they would do things differently.'

"Angelo never did say that he believed Rudy paid, only that fifteen dollars wasn't enough to worry about. I felt that wasn't the point, but Val's calling stopped my crying. It didn't satisfy Rudy though. He wrote Angelo asking for a written apology and I don't know what else. I don't think he's going to get it. Several days have elapsed already.

"So what happened to put him on *your* shit list?" I asked Terry.

"About five years ago six of us women went there for dinner," she began. "We were through and ready to get up, but one of the women couldn't find her coupon. At that time there was a buy one, get one free coupon in the Entertainment Book. We were fiddling around looking on the floor on either side of our feet and saying to her, 'Did you look in your purse? Is it in your chair?' Whatever. Pretty soon Angelo came over and said, 'If you ladies are through, I'd appreciate it if you'd leave. I can use the table for someone else.' It was so rude I'd never go there again."

I was shocked. Now I regret all the tears I shed. I don't care if he believes me or not.

January 12

A violent snowstorm began yesterday afternoon and raged all night. It paralyzed the city. No traffic allowed. The northern suburbs were traversable only by dedicated workers and fools. Bernadette, the weekend receptionist, made it in. I feel she's in the first category. Her husband opts for the second.

It was a Saturday, but Cindy, the head of housekeeping, also came in to help out wherever she could. One of the ways she could was to pass trays in the dining room at lunchtime. She set down Rose's tray in front of her and said, "Do you want me to put the cream in your coffee, Rose?"

"Oh, yes, honey. Bless you. You're a saint," said Rose.

"Thanks." Cindy was appreciative. "I could use a blessing."

Cindy brought the fourth tray over and set it before Rose's tablemate.

"How come I don't have a cookie?" asked Rose. "Everybody else has a cookie."

"Well, it says on your tag here you're diabetic. You can't have cookies," explained Cindy. "But look at this nice dish of fruit you have."

Rose turned hostile. "Why, you somanabitch! I'm gonna tell my son Joey youse treat me like an ass," she spewed.

From saint to son of a bitch in less than a minute and a half. Could be a record.

Doug has a four-wheel-drive vehicle, so he picked up the aides and nurses where necessary, and took them home again. He did this for all shifts. Oh, to be young and hearty again! Sixty-one is young when you're seventy-six.

January 13

Today the world is bleak. Joan died last night. She's been my roommate for only two years, but she wound herself around my heart. She had the most beautiful disposition of anyone I've ever met. She was the one with Parkinson's disease and the leg amputation. She'd been sick for about a month. Slept constantly. She had a fever, so I thought that explained it.

About a week ago she began to ask for pain pills again, so I said, "Joan's getting better." Three days later she started sleeping again. Yesterday she was unresponsive. Last night Amelia, her dear friend, called the priest. Joan died around midnight. I was in a state of disbelief for ten hours, then the tears came.

I find it irritating when someone says, "Are you all right?' Of course I'm all right. When someone you've been close to dies, you express grief by crying. What does "all right" mean? What would happen to me if I weren't all right? How would I know? How do people who aren't all right act or feel? Please, just let me cry when I feel the need.

January 26

The wind raged all night. I can't think of a cozier feeling in the whole world than to be inside a sturdy building with the wind roaring outside and know you don't have to go out in it. Now I think I know how the three little pigs felt when they hit upon the brick solution for their house.

If only every storm came with a brick house.

January 27

Rudy left for Florida last week. He alternates weeks between Nancy's house and Kathy and her husband John's house and is usually gone about seven weeks.

Thelma is bored. She has a cataract and can't read. It will be operated on in about ten days, but in the meantime the aides tell me she says nasty things about me when she gets back to her room after our pinochle games. The latest was something like, "Jean's not going to worry about me [when Rudy's gone]. She's too much in love with herself. I'm not going to put myself out to entertain her." What an uncharitable attitude I have.

I don't blame her for being out of sorts. She almost never wins.

January 28

Rebecca asked me if I had a good movie she could show to the residents this afternoon. I said, "Yes, *An Eye for an Eye* is my latest." It was great, but there is a rape and murder of a teenage girl near the beginning. I told her it didn't show the actual rape and murder, just the girl screaming and her head being knocked against a tabletop and things flying around the room so that the implication was clear. We decided it would be okay.

I had forgotten a few things. The language was pretty raunchy at times. I was playing cards when I heard Rebecca scream, "JEAN!" There was a second rape and murder that I had forgotten about, and this one was much more graphic than the first. I noticed everyone was paying close attention. Sometimes they fall asleep during movies, but not this time.

After it was over we polled some of the residents. Angeline didn't like it too much. She doesn't like violence, but Cliff said, "It was good!" with enthusiasm. Even Maude, our most neurotic resident, surprised me. She thought it was pretty good. Apparently people in their eighties and nineties don't need as much psychological protection as the administration thinks.

February 6

I should be ashamed of myself. Herb called yesterday to say that he and Sophia would be over to play pinochle at two thirty. They come over every second or third Wednesday. I wheeled down to the activities room and asked Wanda to ask Thelma if she wanted to play. She did, of course. Then I asked Wanda to go back and tell her to be down at two thirty, not the regular three o'clock.

When Herb and Sophia got here we waited in the dining room till quarter of three, but Thelma still wasn't there. I asked an aide to go to her room and bring her down.

"Gee, I didn't know anything about it" was her greeting.

"Waddya mean, you didn't know anything about it?" was my cordial reply. "You told Wanda you'd be here."

"I didn't see Wanda," she said.

"She asked you this morning."

"Well, I don't remember." She looked puzzled.

"She came in your room twice, once to ask if you wanted to play, then she came back to tell you the time."

Her face was a mask of bewilderment. About that time Wanda stopped by our table. I asked her to corroborate for Thelma's benefit, which she did.

"I must have been in a fog," she muttered, still searching for an explanation.

After we finished playing I stayed at the table because it was near suppertime. Twenty minutes later they wheeled Elise (my tablemate) up to the table. Her first words, in her Parkinson's-weakened voice, were, "I'm sorry I couldn't play cards, Jean. I forgot about my hairdresser's appointment."

I looked at her dumbfounded.

It hit me. "Ohmigawd!"

"I promised you I would, but I forgot I had to get a permanent."

Here I had Thelma thinking she was losing her marbles, and it was Elise's room Wanda had gone to. The right thing to have done would be to have gone to Thelma and apologized.

But right now I feel I'm getting a little revenge, and I'm going to hold off until I'm uncomfortable with it.

It may take a while. It's been a tough month.

17

Pinochle Partners

February 10, 1997

FLORENCE AND I WERE doing our routine this morning because she forgot to bring a book in for me. (Florence was the cute little gray-haired nurse involved in the African violet fiasco.) She went into a detailed explanation of why she had forgotten to bring the book she had promised me. I exaggeratedly pouted and cried in disappointment. She was exaggeratedly remorseful.

We broke into laughter at the same time. She said, "When we die and go to heaven, I hope we find each other and can stay with each other." Years ago we founded a "mutual admiration" society. This is one of its manifestations. What a beautiful way to start the day!

February 11

Tracey stopped by with some of her mother's spaghetti salad for me. She quit her job here a few weeks ago so she could have some free time before graduation in May, when she will be a full fledged RN. She will still tape Saturday night HBO movies for me when there's something I want.

Cindy brought me one of her famous stuffed green peppers this morning. What a feast. Mama Mia!

February 12

Beautiful, mild-mannered-but-still-fun Cecile was my assigned aide for the day. We were chatting while she was getting me dressed. She commented that she was afraid that Sean was going to quit or be fired because his attendance record was so poor lately. He is a good aide.

I said, "It figures. He owes me six dollars."

"You didn't!" she said with a sideways glance.

"I did," I admitted sheepishly.

She took three dollars out of her pocket and dropped it into my purse.

"If he pays you back, you can pay me back."

I protested. She insisted. I protested some more. She insisted some more.

Her sister works here too. She's on the north wing. She is of smaller build but has the same pretty face. A few weeks ago when she was out shopping, she saw a pair of light blue earrings she thought I would like, so she bought them as a gift for me. I've never seen the slightest sign of sibling rivalry between them—teamwork all the way.

February 13

THE STATE stopped in to check on our problem area. It has been corrected, so we passed the assessment.

February 15

Our Valentine party yesterday was great. A male-female duo sang, accompanied by a pianist and a drummer. They were retired professionals. They charged only sixty dollars, which is not bad for their degree of expertise. I hope we have them again soon.

The staff passed around cupcakes, cookies, chocolate candy, and punch. I succumbed again. There was nothing special about it. The cookies were so-so. If chocolate doesn't have nuts in it, what good is it? I ate it anyway. The cupcakes were made from a mix. I don't particularly care for commercial mixes, and commercial frosting is the pits. I was keeping house in the era when baking from scratch was the norm and mixes were just coming into vogue. My peers and I wouldn't have considered anything but homemade frosting. But those cupcakes always *look* so damn good!

Today the girl scouts came with homemade valentines and cupcakes. Is it a plot to drive me mad?

February 17

Thelma had her cataract operation four days ago. It still hasn't healed. She feels lousy.

Angeline, one of our regulars in the activities room at night, has been in the hospital for over two weeks. She has congestive heart failure, and I think this might be the final time.

February 18

Thelma was taken to the hospital two nights ago. She was completely disoriented. The diagnosis is pneumonia. I don't see the convergence between the diagnosis and the symptoms, but what do I know?

February 21

Angeline died a little after three o'clock this afternoon. What a loss to us. The activities department in the evening is a geriatric hangout, equivalent to Arnold's soda shop in the

Archie comic books. We drink coffee, eat cookies or cake, tell jokes, and just shoot the bull. Angeline's daughter, Toni, is there with her mother every night. Toni is such fun. There's a lot of laughter when she's in a group. The depth of our loss is immeasurable.

I guess I should also feel some guilt now. I'll tell you why. A couple of years ago my sister called and told me one of my Pennsylvania cousins was coming up for the weekend with his new wife. We planned to meet for brunch on Monday at the Greek restaurant down the street before they left for home. Angeline's daughter Toni used to be a hairdresser, so on impulse I asked her if she would cut my hair. I would pay her, of course, I said. I hadn't seen my cousin in about five years, and I wanted to look my best. She said sure, and we made a date for the following Saturday. Toni said she'd curl it too.

I had a feeling Angeline might object, but Rosalia said, "Why should she, if you pay Toni?" The next day Toni said she was sorry, but she had to work on Saturday.

She didn't say anything the next week about making another date. So I said to her, "Are you interested in cutting my hair?" She said she couldn't because she didn't know what her work schedule would be.

Oh oh, I thought, what an idiot I am. I knew for sure then that Angeline had objected. I had sensed she was a possessive mother, and I felt instinctively that she wouldn't want Toni taking care of someone else's hair, payment or not. One of the aides washed it and put it in curlers the day before the breakfast instead, and it looked lovely. I was glad it wasn't cut.

Anyway, since this was in November, and Rudy had gone to Florida, there was no card game. I figured I would play bingo the night before Thanksgiving, hoping to win and rile Angeline a little since I wasn't one of the gang that plays regularly. I did win—two games and the cover-all. I could see Angeline was mad.

I'm not proud of this desire for revenge. Why would I think it felt good to piss off an old woman in a nursing home? Putting it down on paper makes the original slight seem even more trivial. Now maybe I feel a little guilt. Even a lot.

I guess I should also explain why I don't get my hair cut at the beauty shop here. A couple of years ago we had an interim administrator while Doug was on hiatus. At about that time our beautician retired. She was a little Polish woman whom I loved. Her prices had been so low that when the new beauticians came in with their up-to-date charges, the increase was a bit of a shock.

The new administrator sent a letter to the families of the residents explaining the need for the increase. I can't remember how it was worded, but he explained that the beauty shop prices had never kept up with inflation, so now it was necessary for a "modest increase." I felt the letter was insulting. I wouldn't call 133 percent and 150 percent increases modest. I resented being treated like a four year old. Near the end of the explanation he said something about the prices on the outside being higher. This is not completely true. Some are higher and some are lower. His letter incensed me. I don't know why I didn't confront him.

February 22

Yesterday's seventy-degree temperature set a record. Then the wind howled ferociously all night, and today it's in the twenties. This week the ups and downs outside feel a little smoother than the emotional ups and downs inside.

February 28

Rudy came back from Florida after only five-and-a-half weeks. He usually stays six-and-a-half or seven weeks.

He had a one-car accident on the way down. He was traveling on the inside lane of a four-lane highway. As a car passed him on the right, he moved to the left to give it more room, and he went onto a gravel shoulder that was graded. In trying to get back onto the road, he must have accelerated too hard. The steering wheel was wrenched from his hands, and he ended up against the guardrail facing the opposite direction from which he had been traveling. He was trapped in a little town in West Virginia for four days and five nights while the car was repaired.

I suspect this may have put a damper on his trip and was the reason for the early return.

March 1

Terry stopped in this morning while I was on the toilet. Her news was so exciting that we couldn't wait till I got out of the bathroom to converse like normal people.

Jessica received a telephone call from a local man saying he had located Robin's mother's name and birthplace through the Internet. The man asked Jessica to send him two hundred dollars because there were expenses involved. Jessica realized it could be a scam, but she didn't think so. Anyway, at this point she didn't feel she had a choice. It was her only lead.

She didn't tell Robin yet in case her mother doesn't want to meet her. Imagine the feeling of rejection if that were the case! It would be devastating. But it's quite likely that the woman has a family who knows nothing about this daughter.

March 5

Marva, my new next-bed neighbor, took off her nightgown last night and tried to crawl in bed with me nude. I wouldn't let her. It's Mel Gibson or nobody.

March 12

Rudy has complained of having a pain above his right hip for four or five days.

"What could it be do you think?" he asked me.

Our director of nursing was nearby. I asked her.

"Maybe a kidney infection," she said. "Call your doctor."

March 14

Rudy went to the doctor's office and was given an antibiotic.

March 25

Rudy returned to the doctor today. The pain was getting worse, and he felt lousy. The doctor scheduled an appointment for him with a gastroenterologist.

March 27

Rudy and I attended a meeting last night with two of our neighbors, Doug, and the architect who has drawn the plans for our new addition. This building has been in the works for a long time and will sit adjacent to the present north wing. It will be a two-story building with the same number of beds as this building.

There is a lot of red tape in order to get acceptance from the state. Our last hurdle is the town board that must approve it.

The architect said the board would probably give us some trouble because they are the state's watchdogs. What he meant by that is that the new building will be more modern and have larger rooms, so the state will have to pay more for the Medicaid residents. The architect says if all goes well, we can start building by October. It's pretty exciting.

March 31

Rudy saw the gastroenterologist, who scheduled a CAT scan of the chest and pelvis for tomorrow.

April 1

We called 911 because somebody was choking, and Jeffrey was one of the EMTs who responded. It brought back a lot of memories. Jeffrey was an aide here about ten years ago. He was what the girls called a hunk. He got his emergency medical technician license a few years later and left here for a job that would utilize his education.

While he was here, he was good to me. He lived in an apartment across the street from the nursing home. One day he handed me his *TV Guide* and said, "When there's a movie you'd like to see on HBO, let me know, and I'll bring you over." So when *The Big Chill* came on I said, "This is it."

He told some of the staff, "Jean's coming over tonight. Come on over."

That day I asked some of the nurses, "Do you think I should take my bedpan in case Jeffrey wants me to stay all night?"

There were four or five steps up to his apartment, but that was no problem. I was much thinner then, and two of them could carry me up easily. The living room was crowded. Nine or ten of the staff were there. They were talking about just having visited a popular resident who had recently returned home because of an improvement in her condition. I didn't know Jeffrey had heard about my joking remark to the nurses until I asked petulantly, "Are you guys gonna come and see me when I get an apartment?"

Jeffrey was the first to answer. "Of course we will," he said, "and I'll bring my urinal in case you want me to stay all night."

I never did get to see *The Big Chill*, but it couldn't have been half as much fun as that crowd in Jeffrey's living room.

April 2

Rudy returned to the gastroenterologist for the report. Things look bad. He has to have a liver biopsy tomorrow.

April 4

Rudy called the doctor for the lab report, but the doctor said he didn't have it yet. Since tomorrow is Saturday, Rudy will have to wait three days.

April 7

Rudy was over here, so I called the doctor. Rudy can't talk on the nursing home phone because it's not equipped for the hearing impaired. I was the one who heard the death sentence first.

"Cancer of the pancreas."

"What stage?" I asked.

"Advanced."

"How long would you say?"

"One to three months."

There was no need for a lot of words. Each knew what the other meant. "Shall I tell him?" I asked.

"No, I'll tell him when he comes in tomorrow. He might have questions you couldn't answer."

I felt a kind of numbness that blocked out the full portent. I wheeled back to where Rudy was waiting. "The report isn't in yet," I stalled. "He'll see you in his office tomorrow."

Today is Peggy's forty-second birthday.

April 8

Rudy drove himself to the senior center for lunch (a three– or four-times-a-week habit), then to the doctor's office. Rosalia met him there. She was afraid he'd miss something because of his hearing impairment.

After imparting the death sentence, the doctor assured him he wouldn't be in pain. "We'll keep you comfortable."

Rudy left without asking, "How long?" Rosalia did though.

"Now that I've seen him, no more than a month."

He came over to the nursing home in the evening. We didn't discuss the diagnosis.

"Are you going to eat at the center tomorrow?" I asked, trying to inject a bit of normalcy into an untenable situation.

"No, they're having pork chops," he replied. "I don't want them. I'm going Thursday and Friday."

We numbly went through the motions of one game of pinochle (instead of our usual three). I tried to rub his arm in an affectionate gesture, but if I touched him I cried. He went home early.

April 9

He called Kathy in the morning. "Come up. I need you now."

Kathy is a psychiatric nurse. She makes house calls. Kathy said she would have to make arrangements for her patients and would be up as soon as she could.

He said it took too much energy to talk. "Just come up."

Doug took Rudy to the oncologist in the afternoon, then took him home and left to fill the prescriptions Rudy was given. He added one of his own—a quart of Ben & Jerry's.

Kathy arrived at eight in the evening, prepared to stay as long as necessary.

April 10

Kathy brought Rudy over to the nursing home at two thirty in the afternoon. At her request I had a wheelchair ready to transport him from the car. Kathy and I talked while Rudy napped with his head on the table.

"Do you want to go home, Dad?" Kathy asked about three thirty.

"No, I just want to be here," he replied.

We parted at four o'clock with a perfunctory kiss, each of us leaning over our wheelchairs so our lips could meet.

April 11

I was still in bed at about nine o'clock in the morning when I heard the lobby phone ring.

Oh oh, I thought, I bet that's Kathy.

No one came back with a message, so I assumed I was wrong. At ten thirty, when I was up and dressed, I called to see what their plans were for the day.

"Mom . . . Dad died this morning."

It was more of a shock than I had expected it would be. He went from driving himself to the senior center on Tuesday to a wheelchair on Thursday. Friday morning he was gone. He died like he lived—courageously, with no time wasted.

Kathy said she tucked him in with kisses at bedtime on Thursday. She awoke at five o'clock in the morning and heard him snoring vigorously. She awoke again at nine o'clock and all was quiet. His hands were cold but his body was still warm. In answer to Kathy's summons, Rosalia went over for moral support.

It's an emotional experience seeing a body carried out in a body bag. When it's someone you love, it's got to be shattering.

April 15

Peggy flew in on Friday night, the day he died. She had made reservations for the following week, assuming to see him ill but alive. John and Curt arrived by car on Saturday and Joe by plane on Sunday. Nancy couldn't come because a back injury she received at work a few years ago was still too painful. Having just spent five-and-a-half weeks with him in Florida, seeing him dead wasn't that urgent.

If funerals can be nice, this one was. Kathy's choice of clothes for him was inspired—his plaid flannel shirt, his navy-blue and white sweater, and his cap in his hands. He had on his Velcro sneakers, which everybody had teased him about, but a foot problem made wearing regular shoes too painful. I live a high-profile life so there were a lot of people there. I have always felt that people say asinine things in funeral parlors: "My, didn't the undertaker do a good job! Doesn't he look wonderful!" But they did and he did. He looked fifteen or twenty years younger. Somehow that was comforting. His sparse hair frequently had stood out at the sides like Dagwood's. The undertaker combed it straight back, and this made it look as if he had more hair. What a stupid little thing to feel good about.

Both Rudy and I had been faithful churchgoers (that's where we met) when we were younger, but I hadn't gone to church since I went into a wheelchair in 1971—and Rudy did very rarely—so we had no pastor who knew us. The funeral parlor furnishes the minister in cases like this. I was delighted to find he wasn't a complete stranger. His wife had been a customer of Rudy's when he had owned the fur shop, and I had spoken to her on the telephone every spring and fall regarding pickup and delivery of her furs. I liked the minister immediately.

He asked if anyone would like to come up to the podium and say a few words about Rudy. Peggy did so, and John did, and a few others. Then a German woman named Gisa came up to the front. She was an acquaintance of Rudy's from childhood. She told about stopping in to see Rudy occasionally and the two of them discussing the Bible. Then I remembered Rudy telling me about her and bringing her over to see me once or twice.

When I had asked her earlier what her religion was, she answered, "Lutheran." But when she started to speak up front, I remembered that she was a Jehovah's Witness. I wondered why she had lied to me. She spoke sensibly for a minute or two, then wandered off into irrelevancy and stayed there. Peggy took my hand and squeezed it. I didn't know if I should interrupt her, or if the minister would, or if she would stop on her own before the embarrassment became unendurable. Finally she stopped.

All in all it was a very nice service. Gisa promised to come and see me. I guess she doesn't know that I won't tolerate a religion that preaches that its members are the only ones who will go to heaven.

Rudy was a paranoid personality and a difficult man to live with, but a coffin makes you forget these things for a while. I have been preparing myself emotionally for Rudy's death for the last four years because his genetic programming indicated he'd been living on borrowed time. No one in his family lived longer than seventy-eight years. He would have been eighty-three in three more weeks. But I found I wasn't prepared. There was the numbness, the disbelief mixed with tears. I guess it will be that way until reality sets in.

18

Three o'Clock

May 11, 1997

I HAVEN'T BEEN TO THE COMPUTER in weeks. Lethargy, I guess. But something has happened that has motivated me to explode.

I have to change over to Rudy's social security payment because it is larger than mine. Medicaid would drop me if I didn't do this. I spoke to a representative at the social security office who asked me to send them by certified mail my birth certificate, my marriage certificate, and my divorce papers. They would make copies and return them by certified mail. I sent them on the seventh and got them back on the ninth with a request for documents that show identity, such as a driver's license or a health insurance card other than Medicare.

I don't have a driver's license or health insurance other than Medicare.

Someone suggested maybe they want something with a picture on it.

A health insurance card doesn't have a picture on it. Besides, this whole thing is being handled over the phone so they don't know what I look like anyway.

If a birth certificate, a marriage certificate that is fifty-four years old, and divorce papers are not identifying enough, I don't know where to turn. I think I'll just write back and say, "Hey, you guys are joking, right?"

May 12

Florence, the cute little south wing nurse who suggested I ask my neighbor to trade violets, barely made it to work on time this morning. A family of ducks held her up at her street corner. Mr. Duck had just stepped off the curb and was beginning to waddle across as Florence approached. Mrs. Duck (I assume they weren't just living together) looked both ways, then shrewdly decided to see if the old man made it across before she entered a possibly dangerous situation with her little ones. When he was safe on the other side, she waddled across with the rest of the family, quacking all the way. Martha, one of our more alert residents, loves ducks, and this little tale just made her day.

I heard another little tale today. I called the social security office. The woman I spoke to said the additional identification requested was for the purpose of correcting the spelling of my name on my social security file. I sent her my bus pass instead of giving her an argument. I'm as dumb as they are.

May 13

I am heartsick. Cecile told me this morning that she is going back to Utica, her hometown. Today is her last day here. She has not been happy since she left Utica. She is pregnant, and her father misses her. (Her mother died eight years ago at the age of forty-four.) She is one of the best aides we have. She told me her sister is moving back too when her kids are out of school. Another big loss. I love her too.

The days have been dragging since my daughter Peggy left. She stayed until May 4— over three weeks. It was a treat for me. She hasn't been here for a stretch like that since she left home.

May 17

A bunch of us went to the Fireside Inn for Older Americans' Day. Matthew, our male activities aide, sat next to me at my request. I wanted him to sit down before Nita did. Nita is one of our most congenial residents. She is sweet and gentle and has probably never hurt a fly. But she drones on and on about trivialities. She can spend twenty minutes telling you about ordering a hot dog from a hot dog stand. Sometimes you don't even know what the subject is.

This gave me a chance to learn more about Matthew. I don't have much of a chance to talk to him while he's on duty because he's running programs then. That means he's in charge of Pokeno or the crossword puzzle or bingo or basketball or whatever activity is scheduled for that particular time. Matthew is tall, well over six feet, and lanky. He wears glasses, which make him look studious, but without those glasses . . . well . . . I wouldn't kick him out of my bedroom.

I found out he's twenty-five years old, and he has a bachelor's degree in business administration from one of our local colleges. I was curious as to why he was working as an activities aide when he had a degree in business. He told me he was raised Methodist and belonged to an outreach program within his church. He found that he loved working with the elderly. He was considering continuing his education in seminary and becoming a chaplain in a hospital, but he had been warned that those positions were few and far between. So he's still undecided about his career. In the meantime, the business world's loss is our gain.

The Older Americans' Day affair wasn't as good as the last few years. We've always gone to Hugo's Mansion, and there the afternoon included a band and dancing. I love to watch older people dance. They have a certain grace that seems to improve with age. This time there was only piano playing during the meal (which was good) and some karaoke while people were leaving. Karaoke isn't that much fun when people are leaving. I'll have to ask Wanda if she has any influence for next year.

May 19

A group of us went to the Greek restaurant for my birthday, which was four days ago. It was nice walking down, but it turned cold again by the time we walked back. Yesterday was Rochester's annual *Lilac Sunday*. I heard there wasn't a lilac in bloom. I don't ever remember that happening before.

May 21

Today was the birthday party for the May celebrants. On the third Wednesday of each month, those born in that month eat lunch in the activities room behind the iron curtain. The menu is the menu for that day with wine and an ice cream cake added. I invited Terry as my guest. We sat at a table for four with another resident and her lovely daughter.

As we began the dessert course, Gisa came breezing in with her niece. She greeted me in her German-sounding accent. "I told you I would stop and see you," she said. She did not know that resentment was still smoldering within me because of her lying to me and answering "Lutheran" when I asked her what religion she was. I have nothing against the Jehovah's Witness church. I just don't want its proponents trying to force it on me.

My reply was rather abrupt, perhaps even rude. "I'm sorry, Gisa, this is not a good time. This is a birthday celebration, and I have invited guests."

I don't know what she would have replied. Her niece answered for her. "C'mon, we'll come back some other time."

I don't know if she caught the coldness in my voice, but I think her niece did. If they do come back, they'd better not start their proselytizing. I fear I will be rude again.

How long will it be before I realize that Rudy's not going to be walking in the front door at three o'clock?

May 23

Rhonda took me to the plaza again. Rhonda was a housekeeper here when I first came here. Then she became an aide. Then she graduated with a nursing degree and now works in another facility. Two weeks ago she took me to the Greek restaurant, and then we went shopping for shoes at the plaza. This time we ate at the Indian restaurant in the plaza.

The podiatrist had ordered me to get shoes. I was used to just wearing socks. I liked it better, but my feet were getting banged up. I can't wear nice shoes like low-instep flats because I have no muscle tone in my left foot to hold them on. So I ended up with taupe clodhoppers. I call them my football shoes—rounded toes, laces all the way up the instep.

"How am I going to wear my fancy earrings with these things?" I wailed.

The compassionate aides told me that the shoes were nice and that they liked them, trying to make me feel better. It didn't work. I knew what they looked like.

Robert and a few of the others with diabolical senses of humor periodically lean down to my eye level and, with a flick of the wrist, assure me, "Love your shoes!" Then they back off quickly before I can smack them.

Rhonda and Kristin, another aide who was her dear friend, used to take me all over in her father's old Cadillac. I was thinner then, they were both good lifters, and the car was roomy. No matter where we went, even if it was northeast of here, we went by way of Baskin-Robbins, which is southwest. We often went to Rhonda's house and played Trivial Pursuit in the backyard until it got dark. Then she or Kristin would drive down the road and get some junk food, and they'd move the picnic table into the garage. (I couldn't get into her house because it had steps.) Rhonda's garage with its shovels and garden tools hanging on the walls and lawn mower and other garage paraphernalia cluttering the floor came to seem more hospitable in my mind than a suite at the Hyatt-Regency.

Kristin now lives in Arizona with her husband and two little girls. Rhonda, at thirty-seven, is abloom with her first viable pregnancy.

May 28

My daughter Kathy and her husband John came back a week ago. They had stayed for three days after the funeral, and then had to go back until school was out. John teaches psychology at the community college in Daytona Beach.

Rudy saved everything from the day he was born to the day he died. Going through his things has been a tireless task for them—but a bonus for me. It's nice having them around. Evenings, we get in a lot of card playing—contract rummy, at which I am not so good—not pinochle at which I am good *and* lucky. So I seldom win, but I don't care. It's just good having them here.

June 2

Rose died yesterday. I am so glad. She was the one with Lou Gehrig's disease. She suffered so much. The supervisor, who was with her, told me Rose knew she was going to die. She crossed herself and said, "I am going to heaven. Pray for me." Then she closed her eyes and was gone.

Thelma was operated on yesterday to repair a hole in her bowel. It's a fairly simple operation, but because of her lung condition (chronic obstructive pulmonary disease), she is not a good candidate for general anesthesia.

June 4

I think Carol (the pretty blonde former navy nurse) blew it for me. I heard some of the nurses talking about some medication that had a loss of appetite side effect. I asked what it was.

"Risperdal," they told me. "It's for psychosis."

It seems that some of the patients who were on it had to be taken off because they were losing too much weight.

Hmm, I thought, what if I could get put on that?

I told one of the supervisors my plan. I didn't know what psychosis the medication treated, but I would act kooky. I could fake paranoid and manic-depressive. Would that qualify? The supervisor gave me her tongue-in-cheek support.

The next day I was reading by the lobby phone. As the supervisor walked past, she made some remark and patted my shoulder.

I recoiled in horror. "You touched me!" I hollered. I thought I should get in some practice.

"Good! Good!" she encouraged. "That was excellent."

The next day, Carol, who believes in being up front about everything, just asked the psychiatrist if I couldn't have some Risperdal. The answer was obvious, of course. The psychiatrist said, "You'd be getting more than you bargained for."

Since the whole thing was in fun, it didn't matter. But I like to accuse Carol of blowing it.

Maybe I should have tried the poltergeist approach. I had forgotten all about it. Several months ago I wheeled into the dining room for lunch, and I heard one of the nurses say, "Well, there've been no more poltergeists, thank goodness!"

I intruded into the conversation. "Whadda ya mean, no more poltergeists? That was my idea and I thought it was pretty good." I knew they were talking about Thelma.

"You!" two of the nurses chorused. "Hey, Wendy," they called to a third, "the poltergeists were Jean's idea."

"What?" The inflection was expected by now.

"Gee," I whined, "don't you guys believe in poltergeists?"

Their look said, *Have you got all your marbles?* But they allowed me to explain. For the previous few weeks, every afternoon when Thelma wheeled to our table for cards, she had a complaint that something weird was going on in her room: her flowers were laying on the windowsill and the vase was in the waste paper basket, or she had put her dentures on her nightstand the night before, and then found them in her wheelchair bag after a long search the next morning, or the blanket she was crocheting was found on Pearl's lap, or the slacks she wanted to wear were in her closet the previous night and now they were gone, or on and on. She always picked out one of four aides to blame.

I talked with all four, and they convinced me of their sincerity when they said they were not playing tricks on her. So to get the blame away from them, I told Thelma about poltergeists. I said they were capricious ghosts who liked to play tricks on people just for fun. There was no more blaming the aides. From then on all her complaints started with, "The poltergeist was here again."

The nurse made her an appointment with Sonya, our staff psychiatrist. Thelma told me that Sonya agreed with her, which I assumed meant that Sonya believed in poltergeists too, or at least she let Thelma believe she did. Sonya apparently put her on medication (for hallucinations?), and the complaints stopped.

I don't care what anybody says, I believe in poltergeists. If they want to send me to Sonya, I'll go. Maybe I'll get put on Risperdal legitimately.

June 7

Thelma's not doing well. She's still in intensive care.

Benny is one of our relatively new residents. Everybody says he looks likes Rudy, but his resemblance to my uncle is so strong that it blinds me to a resemblance to anyone else. He apparently has Alzheimer's disease. He wanders through the building, often thinking he has some sort of responsibility. Today he thought he was a furniture mover and that he worked in the physical therapy room.

Mary Lou, one of the physical therapy aides played along with him in order not to frustrate him. At the same time she had to get him out of the way. Around mid-morning, she said, "C'mon, you've been working pretty hard. It's time for a break," then led him to the dining room. She got a slice of bread and butter and a glass of juice and told him to sit and take a break. Shortly he was back in the physical therapy room again.

"Hey," he hollered to Mary Lou, "is that the drive-thru?" pointing to the kitchen.

"Yes," she acknowledged since that was the answer that wouldn't require any explanation.

"Well, I hope ya didn't pay for this sandwich yet," he warned. "They forgot to put the meat in it."

June 8

Today is the first day I've been able to think of those words, "Mom, Dad died this morning," somewhat dispassionately. I could accept it intellectually but my emotional self wasn't ready for acceptance when Kathy said them. If he had been sick and declined gradually over a period of a few months, I think it would have been easier. But he was such a vigorous and energetic person, even up until the last few weeks.

I would often repeat the words in my mind that Kathy said to me on the morning of April 11 and feel the same emotions I felt then: numbness, groping for comprehension. Now I guess I accept that he's gone.

June 9

An aide came in and told me that Mac was kind of leaning over in his wheelchair as she was coming down the hallway. She asked him, "What's the matter, Mac?"

His reply defined the problems of a host of us. "Aw," he said, "my front end doesn't coincide with my back end."

June 10

Kate just came in and told me that Thelma died last night. She was eighty-eight years old. She had lived longer than most people can expect to live. Because of the condition of her lungs, this should not have been a surprise. But I am affected more deeply than I had expected to be. Nine months ago the four of us—Mildred, Thelma, Rudy, and me—had a daily pinochle session. Even after Mildred's stroke, Thelma, Rudy, and I played three-handed with an occasional fourth. It's the end of an era.

June 12

Kathy and John left for home this morning. Kathy still can't access Rudy's safe deposit box where the original copy of his will is. The lawyer who drew up the will and both witnesses are dead, and this has presented obstacles. It looks as if her lawyer will be able to handle it from here on though, so I guess I won't see Kathy and John till next year. That's okay, just as long as everybody remains well and happy.

June 14

We had the Father's Day party yesterday. It's much different than the Mother's Day party. On Mother's Day we have tea sandwiches on colored bread (no crusts—I'm talking dainty), tiny cupcakes, and punch. The Father's Day celebration is macho—pizza, beer, and this year we had a belly dancer. The men were watching the dancer, and I was watching the men. Oh, boy, they live in a nursing home, but they're not as old as they look.

June 17

Trixie was telling me this morning about her ongoing problems with her sort-of foster child.

"There's a name for a person who doesn't know right from wrong," I said. "I don't think its 'sociopath.' I'll ask the psychiatrist what it is."

I wheeled down to Laura at the nurses' station. "When is Sonya coming in?" I asked.

"Tomorrow."

"Well, I'd like to see her. I want to find out the name for a person who doesn't know right from wrong."

Without hesitation, Laura answered, "Teenager."

Merriam-Webster, you need to hire this woman.

June 18

We had the volunteers' appreciation dinner last night. The weather allowed us to eat in the backyard, but just barely. There was a feel of rain in the air. That's the kind of weather I like.

I missed one of the best parts. I hope the other guests did too. Rosalia told me that she glanced out the window around seven thirty, and there was Benny with his pants down around his knees peeing in the lilac bushes. Al (head of maintenance) saw him too, but by that time Benny was through and pulling his pants up. The nearest dinner table was only about twenty-five feet away from the lilac grove (as we call our cluster of five bushes), so it's likely that some of the guests saw him. If so, I hope the men saw the humor in it, and I hope the women realized that men think that as long as they have those handy little gadgets they might as well use them to pee in the woods.

I saw Sonya this morning and asked her my question. She said someone who doesn't know right from wrong is a psychopath. She volunteered the information that there is no common denominator among them. Some of them come from abusive families, some come from happy families, and in most cases, every other family member is normal. A sociopath is one who knows right from wrong but has no conscience. Sometimes I feel like one of those people.

19

Diversions

June 20, 1997

THERE ARE FADS in grammar as well as in clothes. The latest here is to suffix every sentence or two with "know what I'm sayin'?"

A couple of days ago I wheeled into my room and got into the middle of a conversation between two of the aides who were getting one of my roommates up. It went something like this:

Aide 1: "Well, I don't think he deserves to come back."

Aide 2: "Don't be too hasty. Know what I'm sayin'?"

Me: I think so.

Aide 1: "If he comes knocking, I just won't answer the door."

Aide 2: "Yeah, but you don't want to lose him for good. Know what I'm sayin'?"

Me: Yeah, that was pretty clear.

Aide 1: "He'll come back. I've got him hooked. Know what I'm sayin'?"

Me: I think so.

Aide 2: "Well, you better be careful. There's a lot of girls out there. Know what I'm sayin'?"

Aide 1: "Not like me."

Aide 2:   "I wouldn't let my Tony go just because he looked at another girl. Know what I'm sayin'?"

Aide 1:   "Yeah, but Noah did more than look. Know what I'm sayin'?"

Me: Yeah. I think I get it.

Aide 2:   "But you gotta learn to turn your head. Know what I'm sayin'?"

Me: Guess so.

Aide 1:   "Yeah, but I done that often enough."

Aide 2:   "I'm just sayin' don't do anything you'll be sorry for. Know what I'm sayin'?"

Me: *Yep.*

Aide 1:   "Aah, they're all alike. They're only good for one thing. Know what I'm sayin'?" (*much laughter*).

Me: No, there I'm a little confused.

Aide 1:   "Yeah, put a paper bag over their heads, and they all look alike" (*more laughter*).

Me: Ah, now I think I'm getting it.

Yesterday I found myself saying it twice. I'm beginning to feel really cool.

June 21

Yesterday a bunch of our residents went to the beach. When I first heard about this phenomenon—I think it was the summer I came here—I thought, the beach! What do they do, pull the wheelchairs through the sand?

It's not like that at all. Years ago, one of our wealthy local families willed its summer home on Lake Erie, almost an hour-and-a-half ride from here, for the use of the disabled. It is set on a grass embankment accessed by a fairly steep cement ramp. We park our wheelchairs on this bank, either under the huge old shade tree or in the sun, and watch the bathers on the beach below. The children especially are fun to watch.

Years ago we used to have hors d'oeuvres of potato chips and Cheddar cheese when we first arrived, but the recent cholesterol-conscious mentality scared us away from that. The kitchen packs us a lunch, and we eat it in the house in what was probably the sunroom. Then we go back outside for more beach watching. (Yesterday it started to rain a little, so they stayed inside for a while and played Pokeno.) About three o'clock, we start packing to come home. By the time we stop for the double-decker ice cream cone, which is absolute tradition—cholesterol be damned!—it's usually about five o'clock.

I turned down the invitation to go this year because I think it would be too hard to push me up that ramp. You'd think that would be motivation to lose weight, wouldn't you? I swear it's like alcoholism.

The other day Henry and I were chatting in the lobby. Henry is ninety-three years old and has been walking with a walker sometimes, but is getting close to using a wheelchair permanently. He is not functioning on all cylinders but enough that you can have brief conversations with him. He was telling me about the wonderful lemon meringue pies his mother used to bake.

Hmm, I thought, wouldn't it be nice if someone here would bake a lemon pie for him? I looked around and my eyes fell on Pamela. She is our weekday receptionist, secretary, and gal Friday. She has a button nose and close-cropped curly gray hair, is a speck over five feet tall, and could lose about twenty pounds.

"Look, Henry," I said, pointing to Pamela, "Maybe she'll bake you a lemon pie. I'll ask her."

He studied her for a few seconds. "Nah," he said skeptically. "She looks as if she could eat 'em, not bake 'em."

I'd tell her if I thought it would make us comrades in the weight-losing department, but I wouldn't want to hurt her feelings.

At least it's not just me.

Pamela's of retirement age but has far too much energy and *joie de vivre* to do so. I have seen her answer the telephone, answer visitors' questions, and work the adding machine at the same time. And take it all in stride. We had a saying during World War II: "No one is indispensible." Pamela may come close.

It's been hot and muggy the last few days, and my 108-year-old-roommate has been saying, "It's cold in here. Shut the window."

If I close my eyes, do you think I could conjure up that Lake Erie breeze?

June 24

Virginia, the night supervisor who had the Russian exchange student living with her, told me that Yma left for her home in St. Petersburg yesterday. She took with her four boxes of our fancy cereals (they only have a few basic cereals at home), three boxes of brownie mix, a bottle of Mrs. Butterworth's syrup, and she spent the rest of her forty-dollar food allotment on chewy candy like gummy bears.

Her parents are divorced, and she and her mother live in a one-room apartment. Those who have carpets and VCRs are considered upper middle class. Everything there is controlled by the government, including the heat. If the government doesn't feel like turning on the heat in certain months, people don't get any heat; they just dress more warmly.

Her mother is a schoolteacher. She makes about two hundred dollars a month. If the government doesn't feel like paying teacher salaries in a given month, teachers don't receive any money that month. I guess they have to budget their income accordingly.

Her father is an architect, and his income is pretty good, so that's why Yma is able to take advantage of some of these extracurricular activities like being an exchange student and still have spending money too. Her father drives a Mercedes. Her mother doesn't have a car. Yma expects to be offered her father's Mercedes when he gets a new car, but the cost of a driver's license is one thousand dollars, and that would probably prevent her from accepting it.

Jobs for teenagers are unheard of in Russia. They don't have the stores and supermarkets and fast-food restaurants that give our teenagers opportunities to work. There is one McDonalds in St. Petersburg, but it's too expensive for the average person to eat there. (Yma has never eaten there.) Babysitting is also unheard of.

Yma says public transportation is excellent in Russia. She wasn't impressed with ours. Almost everyone has a *dacha* in the mountain where they go during the summer months. It's just a basic one-room cabin, no plumbing. Dental care is very poor because of the materials dentists have to work with. Yma had all her fillings redone while she was here.

She was impressed with our array of foods. At home they eat mostly fish, potatoes, cabbage, bread, and cottage-type cheeses. The average life expectancy for men is fifty-five and for women, somewhere in the sixties. With a limited diet like that, I can see why.

June 28

Terry called. Robin's mother has been located. She lives in Tennessee and, just as I thought, she has a husband and two children, ten and twenty years old, who know nothing about her first child. Jessica (Robin's adoptive mother) communicates with Robin's birth mother through the head of the California agency who located her. The birth mother says she wants to talk to Robin, but she wants to talk to Jessica first. She's nervous about telling her present family, and she's concerned about the chances of her other two children getting multiple sclerosis.

July 3

A week ago, six of our residents went to the senior Olympics. Every year, in one of our large parks, senior citizens in the area participate in athletic competitions geared to their abilities. I don't know what all of the events are, but some are basketball, bowling, beanbag toss, softball, and ring toss. The county organizes the event. Gold, silver, and bronze medals are presented to the winners, some of whom are just as proud of them as if they were the real McCoy.

Some from our group have won before, but not this year. What a bunch we had. Cliff, who is completely with it as far as I can tell and is usually cooperative, started insisting at noon that he wanted to get on the bus and go home. Departure time was two thirty, so that meant two and a half hours of cajoling and stalling by Rebecca (the accompanying activities aide).

Maude, who is a tiny thing under five feet tall, can do more damage than a stick of dynamite. She was in a belligerent mood that day. She kept slamming the ball on the ground when it came her turn to participate in the basket throw. The referee counted these fits of temper as legitimate tries, so that blew our chance. Maude also bent the accompanying aide's thumb back, so the aide has been in pain all week. And Wanda's been out all week with a painful back because of an injury she received while trying to lead Maude out of the bus. (Don't forget, we're talking about a dynamo under five feet tall.) Wanda had her hand in Maude's when Maude suddenly jerked it away. This twisted Wanda's body around, hitting her back against the bus door.

I guess the rest of the participants were cooperative enough, but none were able to snag a medal, so we lost out this year. I would never go to an event like that. It's okay if you like the sun, but I wouldn't sit in the sun for three hours to see the president—or even Tom Cruise.

Speaking of people getting injured brings up the subject of nursing home abuse. It still exists, but now the shoe is on the other foot. Several years ago I wrote a letter on this subject to our local paper. Some of our residents bite and kick and scratch and pinch and punch the staff. The victims may not retaliate, of course. They must try to calm the perpetrator with words. This would be difficult for me. I could never work in a nursing home. Thank goodness others can and do.

July 5

I had fresh strawberries for breakfast this morning. Rudy used to bring me a lot of goodies, and people like Pamela are filling the gap. Cindy and a gal from the kitchen staff brought me cherries. Another gal from the kitchen, Tammy, does a lot of my shopping, including buying chamomile tea. I was worried about that one because Rudy went out of his way to get it at the co-op, but Tammy found it at the supermarket, and it's two dollars a pound cheaper—twelve dollars versus fourteen dollars. It's an important part of my daily intake because it prevents urinary tract infections (UTI).

I used to get urinary tract infections every six to nine months. This is the norm in MS patients. A reflexologist told me to drink chamomile tea every day to prevent them. I started drinking it on April 1, 1977, and I've had only one UTI since then. I think that one UTI was because the chamomile tea I was drinking at the time wasn't strong enough. When I told the doctor who founded the Buffalo General Hospital clinic about this, he shook his head and said, "It won't work." (It already had been working.) When I told my neurologist about it he said, "It probably changes the pH balance and makes an inhospitable environment for bacteria." No matter what anybody says, the bottom line is, "Never argue with success."

July 6

Four men sit at the dinner table behind mine. Yesterday I was reading the paper while waiting for the trays to be passed when the conversation behind me caught my attention:

Ray: "How much is it for a streetcar?"

John: "I don't know. About a dollar, I think."

Ray: "Oh, I mean for just five or six blocks. I don't live here. I just sleep here once in a while. I live with my mother."

John: "You live with your mother, and you're ninety years old?"

Ray: "Yeah, but I don't think it'll be long. She's pretty weak."

I mentioned before that almost all of our dementia residents refer to their mothers. They say, "I have to go see my mother. She's in the hospital," or "My mother is sick," or "I have to call my mother—she doesn't know where I am." But what's equally interesting is how few refer to their fathers. I think that's probably because, at the time these older folks were young, it was the mother who took care of the house and the children while Papa was earning the bacon. (My husband never changed a diaper.) Today households are run differently in a lot of—maybe most—cases. Because of the necessity for two paychecks, the father has to help with the housework and the children. I suspect that fifty years from now, nursing home residents will be just as concerned about their fathers as about their mothers. But for now, it's just the mothers.

July 10

Monica came in this morning to bawl me out about *her* mother. Monica is one of our prettiest nurses. She has caramel-colored skin and a nice amount of meat on her bones. She is very intelligent, and she has a beautiful singing voice, which she uses joyously as she goes about her work when she's on the night shift (meaning when no visitors are here).

She has been picking up my teasing-insult sense of humor. If one of the aides, nurses, or director of nursing says, "Morning, Jean, how are you this morning?" I will often reply, "I don't think that's any of your business." It is their business, of course, so I'm assuming my attempt at humor is obvious and they won't take offense. (I don't say that to other staff members because it isn't necessarily their business, and it would come across as nasty.) Or if someone says, "Gee, my hair looks terrible this morning," I might glance up and say, "You're right, it does."

Monica has started employing this type of sarcasm, and I've been commending her. "Good, good," I'll say, "I think you're getting it."

Her mother is a beautician with a shop in her home. When Monica started practicing her newly acquired art on the customers, her mother said, referring to me, "I think you should stay away from that woman."

Not everyone appreciated Van Gogh's art right away, either. Not even his mother. Know what I'm sayin'?

20

It's Not a Tragedy

July 13, 1997

SOMETHING HAS HAPPENED that I wasn't going to put into this book because of the distasteful nature of the episode. But it has become such an important element in my life, I feel that it must be included. To give you background:

After I was divorced from Rudy and after I had a disability income from Social Security, I had my engagement ring put into a new setting with two smaller diamonds on each side. I wore it night and day until my weight gain made it too tight, which was four or five years ago. I took it off and gave it to Rudy for safekeeping. When he died on April 11, I took it back, planning to give it to Peggy for Christmas. I put it in the zipper wall compartment of my purse. (Every woman's purse contains this compartment.) I told no one that it was there. I knew I was going against nursing home policy. Everyone is warned to keep nothing of value in his or her possession. But I thought it would be for just a short time—I planned to have it downsized as soon as the opportunity came for me to get to the plaza.

On the evening of Tuesday, June 24, Sabrina, a former aide to whom I remain close, came over to visit. I opened the zipper compartment and showed her the ring. There was no one in the room but Rosalia, Sabrina, and me. They "oohed and aahed" over it for a minute, then I put it back into the compartment in my purse.

The lunch bunch was planning on eating supper at the seafood restaurant on Monday, June 30. I was going to have to arrive before anyone else because of the bus schedule. The thought occurred to me that someone could snatch my purse while I was sitting there alone, so on Friday, June 27, I opened the zipper compartment to give the ring to Rosalia to keep for a few days. But it wasn't there. Rosalia searched my purse for twenty minutes, even tearing the lining so she could reach into every nook and cranny.

I dreaded telling Peggy, but there was no way out. We cried for a minute, but then I tried convincing both of us it was only a bunch of carbon. "It's not a tragedy," I said. "There are mothers and fathers in Children's Hospital whose babies are dying. That's a tragedy. This is a 'too bad.'"

I dreaded telling Doug too. When I did tell him, predictably he said, "Why didn't you give it to Therese? It would have been locked up where it was safe."

The days went on, and I vacillated about calling the police. I figured they wouldn't do anything because I didn't have any papers on it—no inscription, nothing to prove that it was mine. I considered calling pawnshops, but then I said to myself, "They're not going to tell you anything. They don't want to take the loss on stolen merchandise."

On the morning of Monday, July 7, one of the aides came running into my room and asked, "Is it true that your ring and your checkbook were stolen?"

"My ring was, but where did the checkbook come from?"

A few minutes later another aide came in and asked, "Is it true that you had a ring and a checkbook and a necklace stolen?" The necklace part was untrue, and at the time I thought the checkbook was too because rumors abound in a situation like this.

Around supper time on Tuesday, July 8, a representative of my bank called and said, "Mrs. Misura, there's been suspicious activity in your account in the last few days. Did you write a check for home repairs in the amount of $525 to ——?" She gave me the name. Of course I hadn't. The alert bank manager had thought it was suspicious that I would pay $525 for home repairs when I lived in a nursing home. He checked the signature and found it wasn't mine. He also noted that there was a gap of one hundred numbers between my last check and this one. Two other attempts to cash checks for three hundred and four hundred dollars were made at a different branch. I checked the place in my bookcase where I kept my unused checkbooks, and, sure enough, the fourth book down was missing. The bank representative came over the next day, closed my account, and opened another one for me.

I had considered the pawnshop possibility all week, each time talking myself out of it. That same day, Wednesday, July 9, I said to myself, "What have you got to lose? The worst that can happen is they'll stonewall you or lie to you."

Two of the aides had suggested two pawnshops to try. The clerk in the first one was very nice. She said, "Nothing like that has come through here, but if it does I'll call you and I'll call 911." She was so nice that it encouraged me. I tried the second one and he said, "I couldn't possibly tell you. We get 150 rings a day, and I have several salesmen, so if it came in I wouldn't necessarily see it. Call the pawnshop squad of the police department. They get a daily list from every pawn shop in the city describing everything they've taken in that day."

I didn't know there was such a squad. I did as he suggested and left my name and phone number on their voicemail. Two hours later Detective Anderle called me back. I gave him a description of the ring—a .78-carat diamond in the center (my engagement stone), .33-carat diamonds on either side of it, and .25-carat diamonds on the outer sides of those.

"Okay" he said, "we'll get on it."

The next afternoon, on Thursday, July 10, he called back and said, "Well, Jean, I have good news. We have your ring."

"You're joking," I said incredulously.

"No, I'm not. I have it on my little finger right now." He described it, and it was mine. And I had been reluctant to call the police department because I thought they wouldn't do anything. Wow! He gave me the name of the person whose driver's license was used as identification, Carlena K.

"Does she work there?"

"She certainly does work here," I said.

"All right, a detective from the burglary squad will be over to talk to her on Friday. Don't talk about this to anyone. No one," he emphasized. I told him she was scheduled to work that day.

On Friday, July 11, Detective Morella showed up around 2:45 p.m. He introduced himself and said, "Call me Andy."

We went into the small private room off the lobby. The first thing he did was to show me the ring. It was definitely mine.

"Well," he started, "I have compared the signatures (the one on the driver's license and at the pawn shop), and they're definitely the same as far as I can see. I'll have our finger print expert check it, and then we'll be ready to arrest her, I think."

"Well, if she did it, she's a pro," I said. "About a week ago she told me her driver's license had been stolen two weeks before."

The day before, she had also sat on my roommate's bed, ready for a chat. We talked about different things, then (I don't remember what led up to it) she said, "Remember I told you my drivers license was stolen?"

I acknowledged that I did remember.

"Could someone else use it?" she asked. "It wasn't a very good picture of me." Our chat ended with her saying, "I don't want to make you feel bad, but I don't think you'll ever see your ring again."

"I don't think so either," I had agreed.

At that point she got up from the bed, hugged me and said sympathetically, "I know how you feel." If she stole my ring, I doubt I could do as good an acting job as she did.

Andy finished getting the rest of the details and stood up. "I'll wheel you out while I talk to her," he said.

Doug called for Carlena, and the three of them talked for three quarters of an hour. When they were through, and she had left, Andy brought me back in and said, "On the physical evidence alone I was ready to arrest her, but after talking to her, I'm not that positive. She got hostile a couple of times which is indicative of guilt, but it's not proof."

"Yeah, if she did it, she sure had me fooled," I replied.

"I'm going to take a few days off next week to be with my family, but I'll be working on the weekend to catch up on some paperwork. I'll have our handwriting expert compare the signatures, and we'll take it from there."

Naturally, there was much gossip among the aides during this time. On Saturday, July 12, Letitia, one of the aides, came to me and said, "Jean, You must understand that we don't like to get involved because we meet some of these girls in social situations outside of here, but I think you should know I saw Carlena give Sheila (a night shift aide) a checkbook in the parking lot and say, 'Here's yours. I've got mine.'"

I understood that Letitia meant they didn't want to be known as stool pigeons. The conversation she mentioned was also indicative of a pro, if you ask me. I remembered that Andy was working on Saturday, so I called him.

"Ask Letitia if she'd talk to me off the record," he said.

She said, "Sure," so I backed off to give her privacy. When she was through she came to me and said, "I'm furious."

"Why?"

"She's trying to involve Nola and me. I'll get Nola."

Nola came over to tell me what she knew. "I was in Kay's Department store with Sheila," she said, "and I saw that she had your bank statement and your birth certificate. I told her she should throw them away—that she'd better not get caught with them."

"Are you willing to testify in court?" I asked.

She was. So was Letitia. I fear they'll back out when their anger cools.

Andy said it didn't matter. We had enough. He continued, "I'll get an arrest warrant on Friday, and we'll pick her up the beginning of the following week. In the meantime, act natural. Don't trust her, but act as if you do."

Letitia told me that at some point—I don't remember which day—Carlena called her on the phone. During the conversation Letitia asked her, "Did you steal Jean's ring?" Her answer was, "I won't say 'yes' and I won't say 'no.'"

Then today it occurred to me that, since my bank statement and birth certificate were gone, I'd better check on my marriage license and my divorce papers. Ordinarily I keep these papers in a briefcase in my closet, but since I'd had to send them to Social Security recently because of switching to Rudy's Social Security payment as a widow, I had gotten them out. And I never put them away. They should have been in among a stack of papers on my desk.

I checked the stack of papers, and my bank statement was in a brown envelope along with the letter from Social Security that applied to it. But sure enough, my marriage certificate and my divorce papers were gone. What good were they to someone else? To get a passport? To sell on the street? Now I'm waiting for the detective to call me back so I can report it too.

July 14 (Monday)

Carlena wasn't scheduled to work over the weekend, but she came in today. The first thing she said to the supervisor was, "I won't work on south wing. I can't take care of Jean when she thinks I stole her ring."

That worked out fine because we were shorthanded on north wing and needed someone from south over there.

Shortly after she started (half an hour? an hour?) she went to the supervisor and said, "Everyone is looking at me, giving me dirty looks. No one is talking to me. I can't work like that. I'm going home."

She started toward the exit and then turned back. "I spoke to the detective. I told him my driver's license was stolen," she said. The supervisor pretended ignorance. Carlena protested even more. "I didn't steal anything from anyone. They should question Sheila. She hasn't been here for days."

What nerve!

I received from the bank a copy of the three-hundred– and four-hundred-dollar checks that the forger tried to cash and also a copy of his driver's license. Some of the girls think he may be Sheila's boyfriend or one of her sons. He's thirty years old and pretty tough looking, but driver's license photos sometimes make even gentle people look that way. It's kind of like the old saying: "If you look like your passport photo, you're too sick to travel."

More gossip: When Carlena filled out her application to work here, one of the aides said to another aide, "I know her and she's trouble."

July 16

The heat and humidity have been unrelenting. You just feel beat without doing anything. I hope to call Kathy tonight and wish her Happy Birthday!

Heard in passing, from one resident to another:

"How much is a membership here?"

"I don't know. I don't belong here. I've always belonged to St. Mary's."

July 18

Deanna, Trixie's twenty-one-year-old daughter, had her baby today after a rugged labor—a 7 pound 3 ounce boy. I can't tell you his name because I said at the beginning of this book that all names are fictitious, but I can give you a clue: If he follows his namesake's activities, when he grows up he will build an ark. But, then again he may not, if we don't have a big flood.

Deanna's boyfriend abandoned her and denied all responsibility when she told him she was pregnant. She was happy to be pregnant and carried it to its conclusion anyway. I envy today's generation. They have so many options that those in my generation were denied. They can live together without being married. We would have been looked upon with dismay, at the least. They can have babies before they're married. Our parents would have been horrified. I would have been too immature to be able to handle such a situation, even with social acceptance, but many now seem to do it with ease.

My friend Rhonda took me to lunch at the Greek restaurant again. We spent the rest of the afternoon sitting in the Elderwood backyard talking. The weather was delightful. At my request she brought me some capsules made up by her chiropractor for the purpose of killing the yearning for sweets. Each one contains 3,000 International Units (IU) of Vitamin A. I was skeptical. I'm already taking 15,000 IU so I'll have to ask my new doctor. One of our elderly staff doctors retired recently and was replaced by a beautiful little female doctor of Asian descent. She's going to test my metabolic rate, so the iodine the capsules contain may be objectionable.

July 19

Andy was supposed to have gotten the arrest warrant for Carlena yesterday, but I haven't heard anything yet.

Today I saved half of my macaroni and cheese for supper. I've never been able to do that before. The macaroni and cheese here is good to begin with, but it's creamy and I like things drier, so they brown mine in the oven for me until it's crunchy. This makes it irresistible, and I usually keep eating it—not because I'm hungry, but because it tastes so good and I don't want to give up this pleasure. I haven't had one sweet all week either. When Ronnie took me off the bedpan last night he said, "You're losing weight." He could tell by my fanny.

July 20

Rebecca was passing out ice cream creations in the activities room: ice cream on top of brownies with walnuts, and cherries and whipped cream on top of the ice cream. She came to my room to get me. I said "No. Stay behind me, Satan, way behind."

July 21

I talked to Andy. I wanted to ask him if there was a central agency that should be notified that my birth certificate and marriage and divorce papers had been stolen. He didn't know of any. He told me he got the arrest warrant today, but it wasn't signed yet. "There's paperwork connected with this. We'll be ready to pick her up on the weekend."

"What if she doesn't answer the door?" I wanted to know.

"We'll break in."

"You can do that?"

"Of course," he said. "Don't worry, we'll get her."

After I hung up I thought that I should have asked him, "What if she's really not home and you break in and that will warn her?" It's a good thing I didn't think of it at the time. What could his reply have been but, "Listen, Jean, we've been doing this for a long time. You worry about your business and let us worry about ours."

The doctor also wants me to worry about my business and let her worry about hers. She said the Vitamin A I'm taking is already too much so I should not take more. She's going to start me on a very low dose of thyroid medication. I have borderline hypothyroidism. That may help my weight problem, but I doubt it. The dose is very small.

July 22

Terry called. Robin's birth mother spoke to her and Jessica about a week ago. I will call her Julie. It was a very emotional scenario. She explained to Robin that she gave her up for adoption because she had no money and she wanted her to have a loving home with both a mother and a father. Pictures were exchanged. There was talk about exchanging visits. Her father is interested in seeing her too. He is still in the picture because he is the godfather of one of her other children. Julie has not yet told her husband or other children so a lot must be done before any visiting can be accomplished.

Robin asked if she could call her "Mother."

"Of course," Julie replied. When she wrote, she signed the letter, "Mother Julie."

Jessica's attempts to bring about this reunion and her willingness to do whatever she can to help them meet each other is a testament to the depth of her character. I wonder sometimes what makes the difference between someone like Jessica, who always thinks of her daughter before herself, and those like Carlena, who put themselves above all the rest.

21

Do You Know What Day It Is?

July 27

I LAY IN BED THIS MORNING listening to the sounds in the
hallway:

"It's time to go down for breakfast."

"Which way do I go?" (This from someone who's been
here for years.)

From someone else: "How do I get to the cafeteria?"

And the inevitable: "What day is it?"

Three or four people ask this daily. One of my neighbors,
a tiny little woman who has a compulsion to close every
window in sight and to turn off all lights, asks this several
times before she seems able to absorb that it's Tuesday or
Friday or whatever.

I closed my eyes and pretended I had no idea what day it
was—ever. Try it. It's like living in a sea of disorientation.
How terrible that would be. I've thanked God for many things,
but never for knowing what day it was when I got up in the
morning. Now I'll add that to my list.

July 28

When opportunity knocks, answer the door fast, right? A
week ago I saw an ad in the Sunday paper for giant-sized candy
bars, two for a dollar, at one of the well-known drug chains that

was changing ownership. I told Rebecca to get fifty assorted, and we'd sell them for a dollar. They went so well in just a few days that I told her to get one hundred more. The salesgirl put up a kick, but Rebecca pointed out that there were no restrictions in the ad. She got them. We have only a few left to sell, and they will go fast. It is the fastest and easiest seventy-five dollars we ever made.

July 29

Andy called me at five o'clock this evening to tell me that Carlena was in jail. "We picked her up this afternoon," he said.

"How did she react?" I asked.

"Very calm. She still insists she didn't do it."

"How soon will the trial be?" I asked.

"It depends. If she doesn't post bail, it will be soon. But if she does, it will be a while. You'll be hearing from the district attorney."

"Ronnie, who has been an aide here for years, told me she was fired from two other nursing homes that he knows of. I presumed for stealing. I didn't think to ask."

"Is anything being done about the forgery?" Andy asked.

"No, I don't know who to call. I called one of our suburban detectives and left a message, but I wasn't up yet the next day when he was available, and we just couldn't connect."

Andy gave me the name of a city detective to call to see what he would say.

July 30

I called the detective whose name Andy had given me. He said the case was suburban jurisdiction because that was where the crime was committed. He also said it's up to the bank, and if no money was lost, they probably wouldn't want to prosecute. "But send me what you have on it, and I'll see what I can do," he said.

I also got a letter today from the district attorney's office. I have to appear in court two weeks from today.

August 1

Maralee (Elise's niece, my editor, and an exceedingly intelligent person) says our case is weak if all we have is the handwriting expert. She says the defense counsel will ask, "Are you 100 percent sure the signatures are the same?" He will probably have to reply "no," and there's your reasonable doubt.

I guess it was fun while it lasted.

August 6

I just found out that my appearance in court on August 13 is not for the trial.

Nola had mentioned yesterday that Sheila was willing to talk to Doug and me.

I said, "Is she willing to testify?"

"I guess so," Nola said.

So today I called the district attorney to ask if we should talk to her.

"No," he said. "Just get the names and phone numbers of witnesses. This is not the trial. Don't try to put the case together for us."

I almost burst out laughing. That is a typical characteristic I have: to be in control. But it's the first I realized that this would not be the trial.

August 15

I've been so busy doing other things I haven't gone to the computer in days. Cindy made and donated a fifty-dollar Barbie doll for us to raffle at the annual picnic on August 19. She bought a Barbie doll and dressed it in a pleated skirt of eight one-dollar bills. The bodice was two ten-dollar bills, the cummerbund was a twenty-dollar bill, her fan and headband were each one-dollar bills. That was not the first time Cindy's made one, but it's the first time most people had seen one, and they were impressed. I sat in the lobby selling tickets on five different days and have collected $136 so far. We'll sell a lot more at the picnic.

I didn't go to court on the thirteenth. I called the assistant district attorney who was handling the case to ask exactly what this was for, as it would cost me fifty-two dollars plus mileage to get there. He said it was to find out what I knew about the case. I said I could tell him over the phone. He said he pretty well knew because he took notes whenever he talked to me. I made sure he had the phone numbers of the witnesses, and that was that.

Terry stopped in today to tell me that Robin's birthmother was coming next week.

"She apparently told her husband?" I asked.

"Yes, she told him but not her other kids yet."

Robin had asked Jessica if she could sleep in the same room as her birth mother when she came. Jessica said as far as she was concerned, she could. I realize this is pretty heavy stuff for Robin, but I hope she doesn't lose track of the fact that it's Jessica who's her real mother.

I have yet another confession to make. I have regarded my latest next-bed roommate Maria as kind of a pain in the rear. She is confused, wants to go home, cries, and tries to get out of bed (which she can't do by herself). I feel it's my responsibility to see that she doesn't, so I spend a lot of in-bed time nagging at her to lie down.

It's funny how one little incident can change your assessment of someone. The other night I was watching a movie about a pregnant woman and two crewmen who were marooned on a life raft in the Atlantic. The woman was sobbing because she hadn't felt life in her belly for several days, and she thought the baby was dead. I thought Maria was asleep, but I found she was watching the movie with me when the voice from the next bed said, "Oh, don't cry, honey. Please don't cry. It was meant to be." So, suddenly, this pain in the rear became a beautiful, compassionate person. I'll bet that's how she was when she was normal.

Peggy will be here late tonight. She'll stop in here around midnight to get the key to Rudy's house. She's going to stay at her girlfriend's, but she doesn't want to wake them that late. I wouldn't want to stay in Rudy's house alone with nothing in it.

Of course, my current reading material probably doesn't help in that area. I just finished reading *A Bed by the Window* by M. Scott Peck, M.D., a novel about a murder in a nursing home. I think I should warn future nursing home residents who may read the book that it gives a one-dimensional picture of nursing homes—except for the murder, which is highly unlikely anyway. The first hundred pages or so relate to the residents' relationship to each other and the staff. After the murder, it's merely the residents conversing with the police and the police investigation. I acknowledge that to talk about the programs in activities—the bingo games, football pools, baking chocolate chip cookies and eating them while they're warm, the bus rides to the county fair, the beach, the art gallery, the boat rides, and the entertainment—would be irrelevant to the story line. Nevertheless, the novel gives a false picture of life in a nursing home, and I wouldn't want to go to one based on that drab picture.

Peggy didn't get here till ten minutes to 1:00 a.m. We had a bad rainstorm, and the plane had to circle the field for almost an hour. What a sight it must have been to see lightning below you.

August 20

We had the family picnic yesterday. Another gorgeous day, but a little on the cool side. Herb, Sophia, and Peggy were my guests, and we played pinochle all afternoon while the band was playing. We had a Chinese auction, which is like a raffle but you buy tickets and put them in a pot for whichever items you want to win. Between that and the Barbie doll raffle, we made $362.

Richard was there, the one who used to come and see his mother every night and always had a funny quip. He was telling me that he and his ex-wife had been getting back together again. He's been divorced for thirty-some years, so I was happy for him. I expressed my delight, then he said, "Well, it's the same old problem—she's still frigid. As soon as we get in bed, the furnace kicks on." When will I learn?

Muriel, who used to work in the kitchen, is here as a short-term resident. She is small and wiry, and I thought she was as healthy as a horse. A couple of years ago her bladder and part of her vagina were removed after a diagnosis of cancer. She has been fighting to get back to a livable degree of health. Radiation wreaked havoc with her bowels, and that's why she's here. The staff is trying to find a diet that she can digest.

She and I have always been close. Soon after she knew me well she told me that when I first came here, she looked out into the dining room at the new resident and said to herself, "Now there's a lady." Then she added, "And then you opened your mouth." We developed an affectionate teasing relationship. Seven years ago, Rudy and I helped to delay her at work, then drove her home to participate in her fifty-fifth surprise birthday party.

She has been sad and discouraged since she's been here. After Herb and Sophia left, Peggy and I played cards by ourselves. At ten fifteen, Peggy pushed me to my room and left. I hollered down the hall to the aides in my usual genteel manner. From the room across the hall came Muriel's voice, "Is that tramp just getting home?"

I never thought I could be so thrilled to hear myself called a tramp. It was the old Muriel. She and her sister sat with us all afternoon, and I think the fresh air and conviviality did her some good.

August 21

Today was Laura's (the nurse in charge of south wing) last day here. She's moving to Florida with her two teenagers. Her parents, sisters, and brother live there, and she finally decided to take the big step.

Sometimes we form such a close attachment with certain ones on the staff that we feel we're losing a member of our family when they go. If we have to make a lot of adjustments when we get to heaven, it's going to be a breeze—because we sure get a lot of practice here.

August 23

Our weekly evening poker game was in session in the activities room when I was called to the telephone. It was Rhonda's husband. As soon as I heard his voice, my heart thumped. Why wasn't it Rhonda who was calling me? Why her husband?

He told me that Rhonda had had a miscarriage the previous Saturday night. She went to the hospital on Friday because of bad pains, but the drugs they gave her were ineffective. On Saturday she went into full-blown labor. I was stunned. They were both devastated. She had been twenty-two weeks along. At twenty-four weeks, an attempt would have been made to save the baby, a girl. He said Rhonda would call me when she was able to talk about it. What terrible blows life has in store.

August 24

A twenty-four-hour bug has been running rampant through here. We have never had any epidemic that has affected so many of the staff. They are being hit like dominoes. So it may take a few days before our candy bar sales pick up again.

We saw an ad from another store in last Sunday's paper: two giant-sized bars for a dollar. We've been stocking up all week. We store them in the refrigerator. I can't believe how much better they taste when they're cold. I never knew that.

September 3

I went to court yesterday. Doug went with me. Our turn was almost last. Carlena was called up to stand beside her lawyer, the public defender. It was pretty cut and dried. They didn't ask me anything. The public defender said something like, "My client would like to change her plea from not guilty of a class D felony to guilty of a class A misdemeanor—criminal possession of stolen property." That was acceptable. It carries a penalty of up to a year in jail. The judge, a middle-aged female, set sentencing for October 10.

We left the courtroom, and just as we got into the elevator, an assistant district attorney caught up to us and said, "Very shortly you will be hearing from the probation board, and then you will have a chance to have your say. Write whatever you want to about the case. They will read it and then send it to the judge. She will read it before she pronounces sentence."

Sounded good.

I wrote a letter to Dear Abby yesterday. No one to whom I've told the tale of my ring retrieval has ever heard of the "pawnshop squad," and I thought it might be helpful to spread the word of this valuable asset in our law enforcement network.

September 4

I wheeled down to the kitchen to get a cup of coffee. As I neared the door, I heard hilarious laughter. Claire, a tall, beautiful brunette who used to work here as a dietary technician, had stopped in to visit. She had just told her old co-workers about her Labor Day trip to the Canadian National Exposition in Toronto with her parents. Rudy and I used to play pinochle with her parents every Saturday night, an evening we all looked forward to. After Rudy's heart attack and triple bypass in 1995, he couldn't stay up late anymore, so that fun portion of our lives came to a halt. Claire repeated the tale for my benefit.

First, I must give you a little background. Claire's mother has had her left leg amputated and wears a prosthesis. She walks with a walker around the house or whenever she came over here, but uses a wheelchair for all outdoor trips. When they got to the Exposition, Claire's father started out pushing

the wheelchair. It seemed to be quite an effort for him, but Claire assumed if he needed help he'd say so. He got through the first mile okay, but after straining through the second mile, he indicated to Claire (behind his wife's back) that it was too much for him, and she should take over. As soon as Claire started she knew something was wrong. She checked and, sure enough, the brakes had been on all the time. Good thing we were no longer playing pinochle. He never would have lived it down.

We may also have a developing romance. On the day of the picnic Rosalia said to me, "I just saw Vivian giving Glen a piece of paper. When Vivian saw me, she said, 'I was giving him my phone number.' I don't know if she was telling the truth or if she was kidding."

And our social worker Kate just showed me her album of pictures she took at the picnic. She had one of Vivian and Glen sitting together by themselves. We all think it would be great if it were true.

I've told you about Glen. His wife Sarah (whom we called Lala) died here two summers ago after so many problems. Vivian's father died here several years ago. Her mother is still a resident here. Vivian lost her husband through cancer a couple of years ago. Both Vivian and Glen are attractive, energetic people, and it would be wonderful if they found companionship in one another.

Something just occurred to me. We don't have one male resident who seems to resent being here. All the crying about "I want to go home" and "I want to get out of here" is done by the women. I haven't figured out why yet.

22

Final Sentence

September 10, 1997

THE QUESTIONNAIRE from the probation board came two days ago. I composed my answers yesterday, then Rosalia made some valuable changes and additions last night. I'm pleased with it. Carlena's lawyer told the assistant district attorney that she's sorry for the theft. Well, of course she's sorry. She was caught. This makes me think the judge may view her as a contrite young woman who probably wouldn't do it again. I tried to change that picture by answering the judge's question about my view on sentencing with the following:

> I would like to see the defendant spend some time in jail as a possible deterrent to her preying upon other exceptionally vulnerable people. The scuttlebutt among the aides here is that Carlena stole a nurse's department store charge card at another nursing home. [I named it.] She was out with a sprained back when someone from the store went over to identify her. The gossip is that she also was in trouble at two other nursing homes. [I named them.]

I also explained about my missing checkbook, bank statement, and identification papers, and how, while I mourned the recent death of my husband, this woman went through my personal papers to see what she could find that might be of gain to her, all the while calling me "sweetie," and hugging me to her breast in sympathy saying, "I know how you feel." I wrote that I thought this woman was a pro who had finally been caught and needed to be taught a lesson. I concluded with, "Stealing from the elderly and disabled is the lowest form of thievery. I would like the punishment to fit the crime, and I would like my personal papers back."

I think I showed admirable restraint. I wanted to say, "Put the bitch in jail for five years." I don't think my assessment was going to change the judge's mind because much of it was hearsay. The assistant district attorney already told me this judge wouldn't put her in jail because she had no record. At least now she'd have a record.

September 12

I've been so tired that all I do is sleep, even in my wheelchair after I'm up and dressed. Maralee says it could be depression. I'm not aware of any depression. I thought I was handling all this trauma well, but Maralee says you're not aware of a clinical depression.

Well, anyway, a week ago I received from Peggy a magnetized seat for my wheelchair. I can't remember what it's supposed to do, but after sitting on it for a few days I thought, Gee, I'm going to have to call Peggy and say, I think you just blew $157, kid. It sure hasn't done anything for my disposition. But now, after sitting on it for a week, I'm noticing two things. I'm not constantly tired anymore. I still don't have a lot of motivation to do anything, but I'm not sleeping all the time. I've started the football pool, and I'm going to have to start selling raffle tickets again, although I'm getting tired of that. Also, my toes had been numb each morning when I awoke, extending even into the balls of my feet. When this happened to Rudy about a year and a half ago his doctor told him, "You have to walk all you can. Nothing will help it but walking." So I thought, Great! Where does that leave me? But after sitting on the seat for a couple of days, I noticed the numbness was gone. I'll need more time to see if it's a fluke.

September 13

We finally found a wholesaler who could give us a good price on candy bars. We no longer have to depend on buying up good sales from retail stores. An activities aide took inventory last night. Tonight the first thing she did was check, and she found sixteen bars missing. Damn! That's the end of the refrigerator. We have to keep them locked up in the cupboard. One of the aides told me she saw two aides hurrying into the activities room when the activities aide was at lunch today. Since they would have no legitimate reason to go there, we assume they were the culprits. But you can't make accusations on assumptions, especially when there's no loot for them to be caught with. I certainly hope it was them though, for they've both been lowered in my estimation, and I wouldn't want it to be for naught.

Muriel's outlook is better, but she still has no appetite. She can't get above sixty-eight-and-a-half pounds. Every afternoon at four o'clock she and I have Happy Hour. She gets a can of my Diet Coke from the kitchen, pours herself about an inch and a half in a small plastic cup, then I drink the rest in the same size plastic cup full of ice. It has become a valued part of my day. If she goes home before I die, it will be another traumatic episode that I will have to adjust to.

September 16

Dr. Wayland is weaning me off Tegretol, and I am scared. I feel as if I'm going into battle with no armor. I have trigeminal neuralgia. I've already said it's called the greatest pain known to man, and I believe it.

Here's how it happened. About eight months before I started this journal, on March 21, 1995, I was hit with lancinating pains in the left jaw, some of which were so severe, I howled like an animal. I assumed it was my lower left wisdom tooth, which had been root canaled about five years before. On March 22 our house dentist sent me to an oral surgeon. He pulled the wisdom tooth at my urging and told me to come back in six days to have the stitches removed. It was a very difficult extraction. When I went back, I told him something was wrong because I had horrible pain. He said everything looked good, but he put in the medicated strip that treats dry socket, even though he didn't think there was a dry socket. He told me to come back in ten days.

I went to my own dentist the next day because the pain was so great. He said everything was healing nicely, but I must have a dry socket even though it didn't look like it. So he treated me for a dry socket—again with a certain strip. He said you couldn't leave them in more than twenty-four hours. I went back daily. Nothing helped.

He sent me to another oral surgeon who said, "I can't give you a local anesthetic right away because you have to help me." After much knocking on my teeth and probing around the face and chin, he said, "Now I'm going to give you very small, localized shots, and when the pain stops you tell me." He gave me a small shot just to the left of front, and the pain went away like magic. And on that basis he diagnosed it as trigeminal neuralgia (also called *tic deloureux*) and recommended Tegretol.

The medication takes a long time to kick in, maybe a couple of weeks or more, and they have to watch blood levels (whatever that means) closely. It's very difficult at this point to reconstruct the pain I experienced. But at first it must have been different because I was able to eat. Later, I wasn't. I lived on V-8 juice for five days and then Ensure. It hurt to drink too. I had to gulp it down fast. Drinking through a straw prolonged the agony. Later I had no pain as long as I kept my mouth closed and my tongue in a certain position. It was the opening and closing of the jaw that caused the pain.

The nerve can be cut, which sounds fairly minor, but it grows back anywhere from a few months to two years. I'm not a candidate for surgery because I can't tolerate general anesthesia.

When I wanted a good meal, I went to my dentist for a shot of Novocain. Then I ate quickly before it wore off. I've been on Tegretol as a preventive ever since. Now this crutch is being taken from me because it's been a while since I've had an attack. I am scared.

Then again, I couldn't have alcohol while I was taking it. Now maybe I'll get a good shot of bourbon.

September 20

There were four winners of the football pool, but Lou was the big one. He is so lucky at winning things that people are beginning to say they're not going to get in it if he's in. So far it's just talk.

September 27

I was just getting used to my football shoes, and the aides had let up somewhat on their teasing. Then the hideous appearance of these canal boats with laces was brought into sharp focus again. Olivia, whom I've mentioned before as one of our residents who's not sure which planet she's on, sometimes shows remarkable insight. I was sitting at the dinner table before lunch reading the newspaper. Olivia pulled up and glanced down at my feet.

"What kinda shoes are doze?" she asked in her heavy Polish accent.

My first reaction was a burst of taken-aback laughter. "Why? Don't you like them?"

"Nah. They look like Uncle Sam's."

I was almost afraid to ask. "Your Uncle Sam?"

"I don't know. He works in a factory."

It's refreshing to meet someone who's open and honest. But meeting too many of them could destroy me.

September 28

Each of our aides is given a particular slot each day. This means that all the residents in that section are his/her responsibility—with help from another aide when necessary. This week Russ was in charge of my slot. I don't want the male aides getting me dressed, so they usually trade with one of the girls.

This morning Connie was stuck with Hugh. Nobody likes to get him up because he's a chronic complainer. No matter what anybody does, there's something wrong with it. *All* the time. Connie knew I was assigned to Russ, so she asked him to trade with her.

"He won't do it," she told me.

"Why?" I asked.

"Because he doesn't want to get Hugh up either."

"Oh, keep asking," I advised. "He's just playing hard to get."

In a few minutes she was back in my room. "He says he'll do it if I give him a kiss."

"WHAT?" I giggled. "Well, give it to him."

"Are you crazy? I'm not gonna sell my body."

"Oh, for heavens sake!" I criticized. "What's one kiss?"

"Well, you give it to him then."

"Well, I will if he asks me, but he didn't ask me."

A minute later she came back into my room, all smiles. "He's going to do it."

"You gave him the kiss?"

"Nope." She was proud of her victory without compromise. "He's just gonna do it anyway. He says I owe him, but I don't see how he's gonna collect."

Connie is one of the best natured aides we have. She is twenty-seven years old and the single mother of five boys, ages one through twelve. She says she's looking for a husband, but she won't settle for just anybody, and the good ones aren't that plentiful. She gets some help from social services, of course, but she works hard to take the major share of the load. She just bought a car and wants to buy a house as soon as she can. She said she just got word that her lawsuit may be settled soon. I wanted to know what that was about, of course.

"About five years ago the police burst into my apartment by mistake when they were on a drug raid. I was at the market, and my boyfriend was in bed asleep. The police dragged him out of bed, walked him down the hallway and made him lie on the kitchen floor for about fifteen minutes while they asked him questions. He didn't know what they were talking about."

"He was naked all this time?"

"Of course, and one of them was a female cop."

"Boy, I'd sue too."

"It was humiliating for him. Then they handcuffed him and told him to get dressed. When he protested, 'How can I get dressed with handcuffs on?' the cop said, 'You figure it out.' He was nasty."

"And what did they do to you?"

"Tore my apartment apart," she continued. "I came home with a bag of groceries, and they wouldn't let me in. My father lived downstairs, so I waited there. They cut all my chairs and sofa open . . . and mattresses . . . ripped everything, even stuck their fingers in my food. I'll let you know the outcome."

"When will you know?"

"I have to go to court on November 12. I hope to use anything I get as a down payment on a house."

October 1

Muriel went home two days ago. She hasn't gained more weight, and she thinks maybe she'll do better at home. She lives with her sister. I think it's one of the medications she's taking that's killing her appetite.

Happy Hour isn't the same anymore.

October 3

The damage Carlena set in motion when she stole my personal papers is being revealed in an ever-widening arc. A woman from the collections department of one of our large department stores just called me to ask if I had opened a joint account in July with Maureen Reger. No, I hadn't. I had no idea who this person was. At the time I didn't make the connection between this incident and the theft of my papers over three months earlier.

Shortly after I hung up, someone made the connection for me. I called back and was put in touch with the woman in charge of the store's fraud department in Pittsburgh. I told her about the thefts. She told me to call the three credit reporting companies—Equifax, Experian, and Trans Union and have an alert put on my account. These calls informed me that there were inquiries from Sears with a fake address, Nynex in New

York City, and a couple of out-of-state banks—apparently for credit cards. Sears has no record of an account in my name, so the attempt was apparently unsuccessful—or maybe the perpetrator just didn't follow through.

My friend Gayle came over while I was making these calls. She chided me for not having called her about this when it happened. She called the suburban police. A detective came over immediately. I answered his questions while he filled out the report. In the meantime Gayle came back with Maureen Reger's address.

October 5

Detective Campagna, another suburban detective, came over in the late morning. Again, I answered his questions while he filled out a report. I signed a statement verifying that I didn't give any of those involved in this caper permission to use any of my possessions. Then he asked to talk to Nola, the aide who witnessed so much. She was with him behind closed doors for forty minutes. I hope it was helpful. Maybe now we can get on with prosecuting somebody. Geez! I'm beginning to sound like a vulture.

October 6

Gayle came over with the "fraud file" she had started with all of the police reports. I gave her the one I had started, which included narrative accounts and letters I had written to relevant people. Gayle said the forged three-hundred– and four-hundred-dollar checks had been cashed. "That's why you had to sign these affidavits. There's no affidavit for the $525 check because he wasn't successful in cashing that one."

I didn't know why I had signed them. I just did as the bank representative told me to. I must have misunderstood her because I thought she said something like, "Even if he had been successful in cashing the checks, you wouldn't have taken the loss; we would." I told Gayle that Doug had looked up Maureen Reger in the personnel files. He found that she had worked here for a month in 1994 and left without notice.

Doug said he had just had a nice chat with Detective Campagna. He gave the detective some addresses that he had asked for.

October 9

I've been writing letters and making phone calls to companies who may have opened fraudulent accounts from my purloined papers. What a nuisance! Oh, well, it keeps me off the streets.

Andy, the arresting officer, called to make arrangements to get the ring to me. He said someone told him that there was a Dear Abby or Ann Landers letter in a Phoenix, Arizona, newspaper that sounded like my experience. He told me the signature and, sure enough, it was mine. It hasn't been in our paper yet as far as I know, but I missed some of the columns. It's a thrill to have your letter chosen for publication by Dear Abby or Ann Landers. I started feeling as if I were famous.

While all this was going on, Lou lay dying. Things happen fast here. About four days ago he said to me, "Are we set for poker this week?" The next day he seemed disoriented and gave some wrong answers to simple questions the nurse asked—Kennedy as the president, Nancy as first lady. Things went downhill from there.

October 10

Gayle called to tell me that she had spoken to one of the city detectives to whom I had spoken about six weeks ago. He told her something to the effect that nothing is usually done about cases like this. "They don't even put drive-by shooters in jail." There are just too many of these scams, especially involving older people, to punish those responsible. Well, at least it's been an education.

October 11

When poker night came Lou was in a coma. He died this morning, six days after he said, "Are we set for poker this week?"

October 14

The damned affidavits kept coming in. I had to fill them out for the credit reporting companies and the local department store where the fraudulent account was opened. There were questions that couldn't be answered by "yes" or "no" or checking a box in my particular circumstance, but there were no provisions for narrative answers. I kept ignoring them while the stress kept building up. Last night Rosalia stayed after work, and we filled them out together. That's one thing off my mind.

October 16

Andy brought my ring back today. He said Carlena was sentenced to thirty days in jail and three years probation. That's more than I hoped for.

23

Hot Wheels

October 16, 1997

I'M EXCITED. For the first time I'm seriously considering getting an electric wheelchair. The wheelchair salesman was over this morning. He's going to try to have one here for me in a couple of weeks to try out. Then, this afternoon, our ombudsman suggested I go to the senior center once a week to play bridge. I'm going to find out more about that too.

October 21

Rosalia walked in for her evening shift, grabbed my wheelchair, and pushed me back into the activities room. She works only Monday, Tuesday, and Wednesday evenings, so it had been five days since I'd seen her.

"I'm so upset," she began, "my poor Christine is stuck with a fifth grade teacher who can't spell."

"Yeah?" I encouraged.

"I went to parents' night last Thursday. One of the papers in her folder was a poem she had copied from the blackboard, and it was full of misspellings. I asked her why she was spelling that way, and she said she copied it from the board exactly the way the teacher wrote it."

"Did the teacher do it on purpose so they'd correct it?" I asked.

"No, it wasn't a spelling lesson. The kids are studying different forms of poetry right now. The class was divided into groups to compose a poem about dragons. Each group contributed a sentence. When Christine recited her group's contribution the teacher asked, 'How many esses are there in dessert?'"

"Well, that probably stumps a lot of people," I said. I don't know why I was defending the teacher.

"Yes, but there were more. 'Pitiful' she wrote as 'pittiful,' 'fuel' was 'fule,' 'sweaty' was 'sweety,' and it was only a ten-line poem."

"What are you going to do, go to the principal?"

"What good would that do? It's not going to improve her spelling. Besides, Christine would have a fit if I did that."

"How did she get through college, how did she get the job?"

"Well, I don't suppose the principal asked her, 'Can you spell?' Besides, she has a lovely personality, and she's a great speaker."

"And on top of that, today Christine brought home a paper that had the word huge in it. She said the teacher said it was spelled wrong and corrected it to h-u-d-g-e. Christine said, 'I didn't want to be disrespectful, Mom, but I couldn't let her think I spelled it wrong, so I got the dictionary and showed her. The woman just shrugged it off and said, 'My mistake.'"

"Well, Christine will just have to tough it out this year and hope for better luck next year."

"Or," said Rosalia brightly, "she could simply grow up not knowing how to spell and become a teacher."

October 26

Harry thinks it's time we started thinking about
Christmas luncheon for the lunch bunch. I told him Rosalia
wouldn't go back to Angelo's this year. I said I wouldn't either
if Rudy were here, but it's not going to hurt his feelings now,
so I'll go. I would rather go someplace else, but there isn't any
other restaurant that decorates like he does—like fairyland.
You feel like a little kid, going, "Ooooh!"

"Why won't Rosalia go?" Harry asked. "They're not
going to remember us from last year."

"Rosalia thinks they will. She said if I were wearing a
cloth coat and walking, she'd go. But she says there's no way
they're not going to remember a gray-haired, old woman in a
wheelchair wearing a squirrel jacket." We both laughed over
that.

"Well, work on her," Harry said.

I promised.

October 28

Doug called me into the conference room and said, "I
need to talk to you."

"I hate it when you do that," I whined. "I always think
you're going to ask me to leave."

"Well, I may if you don't cooperate. I've had complaints
from some of the residents and their families that having your
window open makes it too cold for them."

"I know how you feel," he continued, "and I agree with
you. I like the window open too, even in this weather. But if
people complain, you can't do it."

I think it was Helga, the little Norwegian nurse, who did
the complaining because I know she has warned the aides not
to open any windows. I admit that it's been too cold at times.

Sometimes I've asked an aide to open a window, then when it turned colder later in the day, I wasn't always in my room at that time to ask somebody to close it.

I've still got my fan set up, so I'll see if I can get by with that. But it's not healthful to live in a hot environment with no fresh air. Dr. Wayland agrees with me on this.

I don't think I ever described Dr. Wayland. He is tall and handsome with nicely chiseled features and a gentle manner. He is seventy-seven years old, and the young girls here say, "I wouldn't mind a date with him." He earned his money for medical school by playing the piano with a band. He sometimes stays after rounds here and plays the piano for us during lunch. I tease him with, "I don't know why you ever bothered becoming a doctor when you can play the piano like that." Having his support on the heat controversy means a lot to me.

Some women can't feel warm when it's eighty-six degrees even when they have a sweater on. I've never experienced being cold at that temperature, so what do I know? But my room is the hottest one in the facility. Many times an aide will walk in and say, "Boy, its stuffy in here." Maralee has mentioned how hot it is too. "It's much warmer than Elise's," she said. We don't know why.

If there were ever an architect who wanted my opinion, I would tell him or her, "The next time you design a nursing home, don't worry about north and south wings. Make one the polar wing and the other one—the far, far away one—tropical. Because if there is one thing older people can never agree on, it's the temperature.

October 31

We had the Halloween party last night. It was restricted to kids under eleven, so there wasn't the melee we had last year. Trixie was there with her three-month-old grandson, the ark-builder's namesake.

"You're not going to believe this," she said, her eyes sparkling.

"What?" I said expectantly. There's nothing that intrigues me more than a "you're not going to believe this."

"I was watching Sally Jesse Raphael this morning and the announcer said, 'If your boyfriend dumped you when he found out you were pregnant, call this number.'"

"You didn't!" I almost shouted.

"Yes, I did. Without even giving it a thought. My fingers just moved by themselves."

"Well, they called Deanna (her daughter and the baby's mother) and talked to her for about three quarters of an hour. Then they called Jafar."

"Oh, my God." This was so exciting. "What did they say?"

"They just said, 'This is the Sally Jesse Raphael show calling.'"

"What did he say?"

"He just said, 'I can't talk now, I'm working.'"

"But how would they get him to go on the show?"

"I don't know," she said, "trick him somehow, I guess."

"So what did they say after he said he was working?"

"They just said, 'Okay, we'll call you back.' Then they called Deanna and told her that if she had any communication with him, she shouldn't let on that they had contacted her."

"There isn't a woman in the world who could have hung up on a phone call like that, no matter how busy she was. I wonder if he smelled a rat."

"I don't know, but they'll keep Deanna informed, they said."

"Wow, wouldn't that be something if they could trick him into appearing?"

November 3

I got a letter from Vicky, my long-time friend, today. She and Dave just moved from Asheville, North Carolina, to Alpine, California, a suburb of San Diego. And what do you think? Dave saw my letter in Dear Abby's column. I can't believe they're printing it all over the country but not here. Of course, I missed some of her columns, but I would think someone would have said to me, "I saw your letter in Dear Abby's column." Vicky meant to save it (she has no idea I haven't seen it), but they're in the process of unpacking and it got thrown out in the chaos. It's terrible being famous and not being able to see the manifestation of that fame.

November 6

I spoke to Rosalia about going to Angelo's.

"You mean Harry's willing to go? I thought he said he wouldn't go again."

"No, he wants to go there."

"I can't believe you want to go," she said. "You were embarrassed."

"Well, I figure to hell with him," I said. "Why should I let what he thinks stop me if I really want to go. If I thought withholding my business would hurt him, I probably would stay away forever. But he's so busy he could get by nicely with half the business he has, I imagine."

"Well, all right." She was reluctant. "If everybody else wants to go, okay. But I sure would feel better if you were walking and wearing a wool coat."

November 10

Rosalia and I won the first and second quarters of yesterday's game—seventy-five dollars to split. Rosalia's "WHAT?" almost burst my eardrum when I called her. It's such fun to win something, no matter how big or little.

"I haven't heard anything from the suburban detective regarding the theft of my papers. I suspect the city detective was right. There's too much of this going on to try to pursue it. I did hear from the probation board though. I submitted a bill for fifty-eight dollars for the wheelchair van to transport me to city court. One of the conditions of Carlena's probation was that she pay me back. I imagine she will have to pay back the six hundred dollars to the pawnshop too.

Doug mailed the ring to Peggy about a week and a half ago. She got it last Saturday. It feels like the culmination of a long project. If Peggy were here, I'd get some champagne.

November 12

No more from Sally Jessy. I guess they couldn't get Jafar's cooperation, by trickery or otherwise. Damn! That would have been some show.

Mae put up her usual objection to my ceiling fan being on at mealtime. She sits at another table, about seven feet away from me. About every other day she asks one of the aides or nurses to turn off the fan. She's too far away to feel its effects, but she sees the blades turning and imagines she's cold. As soon as she opens her mouth, I light into her, and then she shuts up for that day and the next. Then she's back at it.

I told Harry we have reached an impasse regarding Christmas luncheon at Angelo's Italian Manor. They have to have a credit card number when you make reservations (probably only when it's a large group). Harry won't give his number, and Rosalia said she won't either. I will, but not there. So we discussed other possibilities, which I will present to Rosalia. Harry and Faith never see Rosalia because she's here in the evening, so I'm the go-between. Good night! It's only one lousy luncheon.

November 13

Connie was taking the curlers out of my hair after lunch.

I remembered she was supposed to go to court the day before.

"What happened?" I asked.

"Nothing," she said. "They told me the lawyers had already been there and left. They told me to come back on December 10."

"So what did that mean?"

"I don't know. I'm going to call my lawyer when I get home. Gee," she said, changing the subject, "I hope it's almost time for a break. I'm dying for a cigarette."

"You should be ashamed of yourself," I chastised—then softened it with, "I used to smoke."

"You did?" She seemed surprised.

"For thirty-one years. I even smoked during my pregnancies. Sometimes I'm consumed with guilt, but, as my friend says, we all did. There were no medical directives then, but common sense should have told us. Today women know better."

"Not all of them," said Connie. "Some of them take drugs and alcohol on purpose so their babies won't be normal."

"What?" I was puzzled.

"They get social security income if they have an abnormal baby. I've heard them say, 'I need money. I don't want this baby to be normal."

The idea was so horrifying I was still in a state of shock as she left for her break.

November 14

We had our first snowfall of the season last night, and it was a dilly. There were a lot of accidents. The driving was terrible. It was too early. People weren't prepared yet.

I'm apparently not prepared for driving this season either.

Linda, the physical therapist said, "I ran into that good looking wheelchair salesman last night. He forgot all about your electric wheelchair."

"I've changed my mind, Linda," I said. "There's no way I could afford it. The upkeep could be astronomical."

"Well, it's too late now," she blithely replied. "You're going to at least have to try it out."

Watch out New York. The old lady has cruise control.

November 15

Two more inches of snow last night. If this is a portent, we're going to have a hard winter.

24

Piece by Piece

November 16, 1997

WELL, THE PROBLEM of where to go for our Christmas luncheon
is finally solved. If Rosalia and I had planned it logically, there
wouldn't have been a problem in the first place. We have to go
on a Saturday or Sunday this year so that her husband can be
home with the kids. We have to go on a day when the
wheelchair van (the government-subsidized one) provides
service, so that narrows it down to Saturday. Rosalia called a
lot of area restaurants and found that very few serve before
four o'clock on weekends. (Angelo's doesn't either.) So there
you have it. Few options makes the decision easy. We're going
to our favorite seafood restaurant. Everybody likes it, so
everybody's happy.

November 21

I usually enjoy having people around, but I'm in a bitchy
mood this morning. I taped *Law and Order* last night and was
watching it this morning. Every time an aide came into the
room to get up one of my roommates she'd say, "What are you
watching?"

"*Law and Order*," I'd mumble quickly with a wave of the
hand, which meant leave me alone.

Then, invariably, "What's it about?"

"Then I'd shout, 'Shut up!'" and stop the tape and rewind it for a few seconds to catch the conversation that I missed. When the next aide came in she didn't know what had just transpired, so the scenario repeated. By the fourth one I really blew. This morning it happened to be Stan the maintenance man. Good thing he doesn't hold grudges.

Then on top of that, when an aide got Stephanie up, the first thing Stephanie said was, "Ooh, it's cold in here. Are the windows open?"

Here I was with the fan blowing on me because it was so hot and stuffy with all the windows closed, and she's cold. If we're both still living when the new building is ready for occupancy, I will make sure she is not my roommate.

And to put me over the top, Gretchen was really wired this morning—as she is at some point most days. She screeched three octaves above high C that she wanted to go home. Of course, there isn't anybody here who wouldn't gladly contribute whatever assets they had to send her home if that would make her happy (and quiet). But she probably wouldn't know she was home even then. I wish I could help Gretchen and the other unhappy ones see that it's not the nursing home that's so awful; what's awful is the process of aging and dying that gets you and takes parts of you away piece by piece. And what can any of us do about that?

I just had some terrible news. I think this news ends my gripe session for the day. Cindy came in and told me that Muriel has a large pelvic tumor. Nothing can be done about it except to try to keep her comfortable. Muriel has had a hard life according to most people's standards. I did her biography when I was doing the newspaper, so I know a lot about her. She was the second youngest of fourteen children. She and her next older brother and younger sister got into all sorts of mischief, most of it involving truancy. Her father got weary of being called at work about their truancy around the same time their mother realized she couldn't cope with her three youngest children, so the three were put into a Catholic orphanage. Her mother didn't abandon them, though. She visited every Sunday with gifts of peanuts, popcorn, or candy.

Even the nuns couldn't make Muriel conform; she was always "out of bounds." By eighth grade, they realized she was a hopeless case and put her to work in the kitchen. She loved washing the dishes and pots and pans. She loved peeling the vegetables and helping can food for the winter. She even liked washing clothes and pressing the nuns habits. About twenty-eight years ago she ended up here as an aide. When there was an opening in the kitchen, she grabbed it, glad to be back with her first love.

Her early years of mischief are probably what gave her the background for being the fun person she is. In spite of what some people might consider a pitiful childhood, Muriel says, "If I were a kid again, I'd do everything over the same way."

I guess you're lucky if you feel that way at the end.

November 22

About three months ago Rosalia came up with the idea of compiling a cookbook to sell at our December bazaar. Today she brought in some of the completed ones. She and her husband did all of the work. Hours and hours of it—typing, printing, copying, laminating, folding, punching holes. Doug contributed the paper, so our only expenses are the rings to hold the pages together.

It started with Rosalia composing a letter to all family members asking them to submit their favorite recipes. This was enclosed with the September statements. The response was very disappointing at first, almost nil. I said I had a lot of recipes to contribute. So did two members of the kitchen staff, and with Rosalia's added we figured we could turn out a cookbook compiled by the four of us. I suggested that we call it the P.O.Y. Cookbook. The parenthetical explanation would be *Plenty of Yummies*, but the true secret meaning would be *Piss on You*, meaning "To hell with all you uncooperative people. We can do it without you."

Gradually the recipes started coming in, especially from people with whom we had frequent contact. We ended up with a nice assortment.

"Gee, they turned out nice," I said.

I leafed through while Rosalia waited expectantly, and again I expressed my admiration.

"You didn't notice anything?" she asked.

I shook my head in puzzlement.

She turned to a recipe for stuffed mushrooms in the appetizer section. Since we had enough eventual cooperation to turn out a nice finished product, there was no necessity to vent the animosity we had originally felt. But Rosalia wasn't willing to let one of our best secret jokes go unacknowledged. The recipe was submitted by Helen Poy.

November 30

We have three fire drills a month, one on each shift. One of the maintenance men blows some kind of loud blaring horn to signal the staff. The receptionist announces "Code Seven" over the microphone. That's the code for a fire. Then the staff goes through the required steps to protect the residents. I don't really know what there is here to burn. The building is brick, the walls plaster, the floors cement. All bedspreads, drapes, and curtains are made of fire-retardant materials. Nevertheless, it's a New York State requirement.

Yesterday we were playing bingo when the honk-blare sounded. Gretchen was in the dining room with us even though she can't concentrate long enough to participate.

"Vats dat?" she wanted to know.

"That means there's a fire," said Cliff. "Ya better run."

Gretchen became hysterical. She turned her wheelchair around screaming, "Mootsy! Mootsy!"

Cliff doesn't always function on all eight cylinders anymore, but I could tell by the diabolical leer on his face that he knew what he was doing this time.

Someone got Mootsy from Gretchen's bed and put him in her lap. Mootsy is a stuffed dog that she thinks is her real cat. When they were able to convince her there was no fire and Mootsy was safe, the crisis was over. But Cliff felt it was a very successful fire drill. It just made his day.

December 5

Two nights ago Rosalia brought me four huge bagels. I was eating one and had one in my lap for later when Nita walked in.

"Ooh!" she said. "Where did you get those?"

"Rosalia gave them to me" is what I said, but *Oh, shit!* is what I was thinking.

"Ooh," she said again with a higher lilt. The obvious translation was, "Can I have one?"

I got the message and snarled in my gracious manner, "If I give you one, will you eat it? I don't want it wasted."

"Well, of course I'll eat it. I don't waste anything."

Yeah, right. She has a small appetite. A Lorna Doone cookie fills her up, and these are larger than average bagels.

So I reluctantly handed her the bagel I was saving for later and hoped I wouldn't regret it.

This morning while I was in bed waiting for my breakfast tray, I heard a conversation outside in the hallway that made me chuckle out loud.

Nita's voice intruded on my consciousness. "Yes, you ate my whole bagel."

"I did not."

"Yes, you did. I'm going to make your brother buy me another one." Nita is a gentle person, and it was a gentle reprimand.

Nita was in the hallway again after I was dressed, so I wheeled out to catch her. "What happened to your bagel?"

"She ate it on me."

"Who's she?"

"My roommate," she said with a nod of her head.

"How did she get it?" I asked.

"I gave it to her." Typical Nita logic.

"Why?"

"Because she said she was hungry."

"Well, why didn't you just give her part of it?"

"I did. I broke off one bite at a time, but she kept saying she was still hungry."

I just shook my head.

"All I got was the last tiny bite," she said making a small circle with her thumb and forefinger. "And it was good. That was the first time I had tasted a bagel."

I must have looked distressed.

"But that's okay," she added. "One of the girls is going to get me one."

And here I was worried it would be wasted.

December 6

Tammy brought me in some more bagels this morning—cinnamon and raisin. Now my good side is struggling with my bad side—give Nita one or not? Every morning she bemoans the loss of her bagel, and she seems angrier with her roommate with each retelling. The aide who promised her another bagel keeps forgetting. I can't wait to see whether my good side or my bad side will win out. It's hard for me to share when it's food.

Tammy has been here longer than I have. She's one of the kitchen staff that has done a lot of my shopping since Rudy died. She's a dear, a short-haired blonde, who is in the process of divorcing her husband. (He met someone else on the Internet and walked out.) She has a cherubic face with a peaches and cream complexion that belies her forty-six years. And, like me, she's struggling with her weight.

Now she has a problem that's becoming more complex. To me it's funny, but to her it's serious. A couple of weeks ago she went into one of the chat rooms on the Internet and became acquainted with a twenty-one-year-old-guy who wanted to know if she wanted to participate in cybersex.

"Sure," she said.

"Tammy!" I admonished, then, "So what happened?"

"First he typed, 'You're unzipping my pants.' He was going to teach me how to play this game." Her eyes twinkled. "So I typed, 'Okay,' determined to learn."

"Yeah?" I prompted.

"Then he said, 'I'm taking off your blouse.'"

"Good night. I don't think I'm sophisticated enough for this," I told Tammy. "Then what?"

"Then he said, 'Now you're putting your hand in—'"

"That's enough!" I hollered. "I can't believe you went along with it."

"Oh, I thought it was great fun. While he was doing his thing, I was laughing my head off."

But, now it seems cyber stud wants her picture.

"Well, send it to him," was my solution.

"I told him I was twenty-six years old. I may not look forty-six, but I certainly couldn't pass for twenty-six."

"If you want to continue this game, you may have to tell him the truth."

"Maybe I'll send him my sister's picture. She's eleven years younger than I am."

Oh, what a tangled web we weave when first we practice to deceive.

It is fun, though.

December 7

Did you ever get blamed for something you didn't do? That I can handle. I fume and castigate the person who did the blaming and enlist the support of my friends and acquaintances and anybody within hearing distance. Then it blows over. But the opposite happened today, and it's a little harder to deal with.

As I mentioned, Rosalia and her husband made the cookbooks for our bazaar. Nita's daughter had left money and envelopes with me to mail the finished product to her in Florida, and to her sisters out of state, and to her daughter. Today I received a letter from her, complimenting me on the wonderful job I did.

She never met Rosalia because she always visits in the daytime and Rosalia works at night. I was the only contact. Her letter contained phrases like, "I was amazed at the quality of the book," "far beyond anything I could have imagined," and "organizational and printing work is top notch." She said she just had to write in praise of my efforts. She said I should be very proud of the finished product.

Well, I would be except I had nothing to do with the finished product but contribute recipes like everybody else. Rosalia didn't think it was as funny as I did. She said, "You were my main support," trying to rationalize. That may be true, but the letter wasn't referring to that. I'll explain the situation to Nita's daughter when she comes back in the spring. In the meantime, I'll just paraphrase Jack Benny when he was given an award he felt he didn't deserve: "I really don't deserve this, but then, I have multiple sclerosis and I don't deserve that either. So I thank you."

December 8

I am sick. I just found out that Carol was fired. She's the former navy nurse. I don't know the details. From what I can get so far, it has something to do with her salty language. She was an upper—so pretty to look at, so much fun, and a good nurse. I feel as if there's a leaden weight in my stomach. I'm not the only one. Everyone loved her.

December 10

My bagels are gone. My bad side won out. I ate them all.

December 18

Tammy and I were lamenting all the things we had left to do before Christmas.

"And I've got to bake cookies for the sick and shut-in," she enumerated.

"Oooh," I said, brightening considerably. "I'm a shut-in."

We burst into laughter simultaneously.

"Not really," she said. "The fish restaurant on Saturday, the Greek restaurant on Monday, and the Galleria Mall on Wednesday isn't very shut-in."

Yes, I had been out quite a bit. The lunch bunch had their luncheon on Saturday. The decorations weren't as festive as Angelo's, but we always have a good time. Rhonda took me to the fish restaurant on Monday. I went to the Galleria Mall for the first time on Wednesday. I wasn't impressed. It's the largest mall in the area, but it's not decorated nearly as gaily as the other suburban malls. Gayle met us there, and we shopped and ate together.

December 21

Mildred looks awful. She has lost weight, and not being able to wear her dentures has made her look twenty years older than she did when we were playing pinochle together.

December 26

Maralee, Elise, and I ate Christmas dinner in the activities room by ourselves as we do every year—except this year it was without Peggy and Rudy. The activities room Christmas tree was especially beautiful this year. We had a terrible windstorm last year that destroyed our storage shed and its contents, so we had to get new Christmas trees this year. They are exceptionally nice, even untrimmed.

Some of the activities directors over the years let the residents decorate the tree, feeling that participation was good for them. That may be so. They probably enjoyed it for half an hour, but then they (and we and visitors) had to look at it for the next three weeks, and it looked as if two- and three-year-olds had done a number on it.

This year Rebecca and whoever helped did it in blue, silver, and white. It is the prettiest one we've ever had. A train encircles its base during the day. That was really a touch of genius.

Maralee had Cornish hens. It was my first time. They were good, but the salad was the best I ever tasted—romaine, radicchio, tomatoes, cucumbers, purple onions, and mild pepper rings. (Maralee also includes arugula when it's available.) No dressing was necessary.

Trixie came into my room in the morning with an interesting tale. She told her ex-boyfriend's ex-mother-in-law that she would take her dog, a black Labrador mix named Licorice, so she could go on vacation.

"Nobody told me," said Trixie, "that Licorice could nudge the gate latch open with her nose."

At three o'clock Trixie found the yard empty. After the initial panic she organized a search party—her four children, Deanna's boyfriend, Trixie's ex-boyfriend, her ex-boyfriend's ex-wife and her ex-boyfriend's two sons, one of whom lives with her family. The other one lives with the ex-boyfriend's ex-wife's mother, who is his grandmother and the owner of the dog. On paper this sounds like a nutty bunch, but they're not. They're an admirable family. They searched until eleven o'clock at night, then, exhausted emotionally and physically, admitted defeat. Trixie went to bed trying to figure out what she was going to tell Licorice's mother.

At five o'clock the next morning Trixie's dog barked. She went into the kitchen and opened the door to let Mason out and there was the runaway wagging her tail. She was gone for over fourteen hours and found her way back after having been there only one time. I think it's amazing.

I still miss Carol. There's a marvelous old saying to cover incidents like this: Shit Happens. Yeah, it sure does. That's why we all need others around—to empty the bedpan when it gets full.

25

Damp Grass between My Toes

December 30, 1997

THIS MORNING, FRED'S MESSAGE was about finishing your personal unresolved issues before welcoming in the New Year. He admonished us to let go of our mistakes, make a comprehensive list of regrets, roll it up into a tight scroll, and put a match to it. This got me to thinking about some of my regrets. I wondered if I could do that—put a match to them.

I always regretted that I never planted raspberry bushes along the fence in our backyard. That one should be easy enough to let go of. But when I think of all the free raspberries I could have had . . .

I wish I'd been a better mother, but nothing I can do about it now.

Why didn't I ever bake a pineapple upside-down cake? They're so good.

I'm sorry I didn't have my ears pierced until I was fifty-one years old. When I think of all the years I suffered with clip-on earrings . . .

I always wished I could dance, but I don't think I could have learned—I think maybe I don't have a sense of rhythm.

I lie in bed now and wish I had made a bed of cultivated wild flowers in my backyard. But that one's fairly easy to let go of.

I'm sorry that I never ran barefoot across a golf course. Can you imagine how that lush turf would feel drenched in the morning dew?

I'm sorry that I never studied wines. I would love to be able to distinguish and appreciate good wines.

I regret that I pulled out the hollyhocks that used to grow in our backyard because I considered them weeds. Now they're desirable flowers.

As Fred suggested, I might try that rolling-into-a-scroll-and-burning trick. But I sure wish I'd run across that golf course while I had the chance. I can almost feel the damp grass between my toes.

December 31

Rhonda took me to the movies last night to see *The Rainmaker*. It was great. I'm an avid fan of John Grisham's. We got there early and my popcorn and Pepsi were almost gone by the time the movie started, but it was okay. They served their purpose. They made me feel like a teenager going to the movies.

January 1, 1998

Well, I thought it was a great idea—the train encircling the Christmas tree, but now we can forget about it, at least until next year. Last night Benny broke up two sections of the track—just picked them up and broke them in two as if that were the normal thing to do. Then he walked away brushing his hands against one another as if he had just accomplished a mission.

January 3

Oh the joys of institutional heating systems. It was so hot in here last night that it was impossible to sleep. I had the fan blowing directly on me and, finally, the window open contrary to orders. It was only open an inch. It should have been open three inches. I thought that was a fair enough compromise. I had somebody close it before the morning shift came in. Then, after the aides took out two of my roommates, they closed the door. I had been napping, and the stuffiness woke me up. We had had five-degree weather a few days before, and then it warmed up suddenly to close to fifty, but nobody in maintenance had turned down the furnace.

I put my call light on for somebody to open the door. A couple of aides called in sick this morning so we were short handed, and nobody answered. So I reverted to my secret weapon. I turned my television volume up as loud as it would go. Then they came running to see what the ruckus was about. Helga was the one who answered.

In my frostiest voice I said, "As long as I can't have a window open, will you please see to it that my door is open at all times when it isn't necessary to be closed for privacy." I was annoyed—well, that isn't really a strong enough word—because she was the one who went to Doug with the complaint in the first place. "It's so hot in here I can't breathe."

"Jean," she countered, "it's hot here, but it's cold in the last rooms at the end of the hall. And there are people right outside your door who are complaining of being cold."

"That's exactly my point." I said. "No matter how hot it is, there are always a few who are going to complain."

"Well, I'll see what the thermostat says," she offered.

What the hell difference did it make what the thermostat said? Everybody was complaining all night. It's hard to work in temperatures like this.

She stuck her head back in a minute later and said, "For what it's worth, Stan just came in and said, 'It's too damn hot in here.' He'll turn it down."

"Well, hooray for Stan."

She went on, "He's going to turn the boiler down twenty-five degrees, but it will take some time for the building to cool down. In the meantime, you can have your window open if the door is closed and you're the only one in the room."

Well, thank you, Helga.

Helga is a little person with no meat on her bones, and I guess she feels the cold more than the average person. But is it wrong of me to say it's not fair to anybody, including the employees, to try to accommodate the few people whose hypothalamuses are so out of kilter they're almost never warm? Doug says the temperature must be seventy-one to eighty-one degrees by state mandate. Well, that's fine. Let's just keep it a little closer to seventy-one than eighty-one.

January 6

I somehow knew Nita would wheedle another bagel out of me, one way or another. I left the activities room at eight thirty this evening when it was time for Rosalia to sign out. She came running back to my room to give me the scoop.

"Nita just said to me, 'Where did Vera get those doughnuts that were four for a dollar?' I said, 'Vera? You mean Jean?' She said, 'Yes.'

"So I said, 'Do you mean bagels?' She said, 'Yes, I guess so. Could you get me some now?'

"I can't get away from her. I told her I have to hurry home because my husband has to go to work. But she said, 'Well you might pass the place on your way home and it would be a shame not to stop.' I can't make her understand I'm in a hurry. And I told her they were forty-nine cents apiece. She insists you said they were four for a dollar."

"Does she have any money?" I asked.

"I don't know, and I don't have time to get into a conversation about it."

I took two dollars out of my purse. "Here, when you get a chance—if it's a week from now or whenever—get four and I'll give her two. Just shout you'll get them when you can and run past her."

She left on the run.

January 7

Rosalia came in at six thirty. I said, "What happened with Nita?"

"I did as you said. I ran past her while telling her you gave me money to get some, and I would do it as soon as I could. She said, 'You mean Vera gave you the money?' My last words to her were, 'Okay, *Vera,* if that's the way you want it."

"I probably won't get a chance till next week. She doesn't understand that I have to hurry home on certain nights because Greg has to get to work."

We didn't have any more time to talk because it was bingo night.

January 12

I called Terry a few days ago to tell her that Gayle told me about somebody with multiple sclerosis who had received a bone marrow transplant with her own bone marrow and was cured. The doctors removed her bone marrow, then zapped her body with strong drugs (toxins?) to kill everything, then planted the good marrow back in. Recovery time was fast because it was her own marrow. It's a dangerous procedure. If it doesn't cure you, you're dead. Terry asked me to find out more about it. I called Gayle, and she said she heard about it on television. She said she would go on the Internet and see if she could find any information.

January 15

I'm sitting here with the windows closed and the fan blowing hot air on me while I'm playing bridge on my computer. Some of the women are sitting in the hallway. The conversation I'm hearing is:

"It's so cold in here. Aren't you cold?"

"Oh, yeah, I'm freezing."

"They don't care."

"Nah, they don't care how cold it is."

"They don't care about us. If they did, they'd turn the heat on."

I think a good stiff drink would help me, but I'm back on Tegretol temporarily (I had one short episode of pain which strongly resembled the pain I had previously from neuralgia), so I can't have alcohol. I could blow my brains out, but that seems a little drastic. Maybe if I just screamed, that would help.

Rosalia brought the bagels in this evening. I've had a chance to think it over, and I'm thinking maybe it was a little rash to give Nita two. To be on the safe side I'd better start with one. I don't want another item to add to my list of regrets.

January 16

I woke up at one o'clock in the morning to use the bedpan. The heat was so stifling I couldn't get back to sleep. I asked Ronnie to see what the thermometer in the lobby registered. He brought it back to show me. It was seventy-nine degrees. Well, that's within the States parameters, so I can't complain officially. I read until two-thirty, then called Monica, the nurse on duty, to make me some toast.

"How would you like some pizza instead?"

"What? Did you guys have a party while I was asleep?"

"No, but we had pizza."

She nuked a piece and brought it in. It was covered with olives and onions and mushrooms—all the stuff I like. It's amazing how the wee hours of the morning enhance the allure of pizza.

January 17

One of the aides answered my call light to take me off the bedpan after breakfast. She rinsed it thoroughly.

I complimented her, "You done good. You're one of the best."

"Well, don't let that get around. People start depending on you then." Then, "I'll be right back," as she left the room.

A moment later she came back.

"Where did you go?"

"I wanted to get some rubber gloves to put on the rack in the bathroom so we don't have to go down to the utility room each time."

"Well, that was very efficient. It was a stupid thing to do if you don't want it to get around that you're dependable."

"But only you and me know about it, right?"

"Yeah, so?"

"So if word gets around, I'll know where it came from."

"And that means there'll be repercussions?" I asked meekly.

"You got it," she assured me as she left the room.

There's nothing like an aide with a good sense of humor to start the day off right.

January 18

I asked Rosalia to give Nita one of the bagels. She was around the corner from where I was sitting, but I heard her say, "Oh, no, it was a doughnut I wanted."

"This is all Jean has," Rosalia explained.

"Well, all right then. Tell her thanks."

I guess I don't have to worry about giving her another one.

January 23

THE STATE came in for the annual survey two days ago. We passed with flying colors. They always interview a group of the most alert and oriented residents on the first day. They use a printed questionnaire that covers everything. When they asked about the heat situation and air circulation, I took the chance to talk about my discomfort and that of others who mind the heat. The state representative suggested putting a thermometer in my room. He said he would talk to Doug and Al, the head of maintenance. I took that as a "Go" sign to open my window a crack if it gets too hot. They asked about the walkers. How troublesome were they? Each resident took turns describing how troublesome they were to him or her. I offered, "What's more troublesome to me are the hollerers," then described Gretchen.

"Okay," the state rep said, "I'll mention that to the nursing department."

"Oh, no," I protested, "Don't say anything. They're working on it. I just brought that up conversationally."

"I know," he said, "but when you get a group like this who doesn't have any complaints, we have nothing to work with. We need something, so I'll just use this as a subject to talk about."

Later, when I saw Doug, I said, "I am p.o.ed."

"Why?" He looked concerned.

"I did my best to get you a deficiency, and they didn't go for it."

January 31

Rhonda called. We're making plans to see *The Horse Whisperer*. We want to get Florence to go too. All of us read the book and loved it. Florence is retired now, and we don't want to lose touch.

By the way, I found out Risperdal doesn't always decrease the appetite. It can go either way. Sometimes you gain, so it's a good thing I didn't inveigle my way into an illicit prescription.

Over the Christmas holidays I ate two pounds of chocolate covered nuts, a pound of pistachios, a jar of macadamia nuts, six homemade truffles (Ooh-la-la), a million homemade cookies, and a few pieces of cakes and pies. Oh well. I spent three years trying to give up smoking before it was accomplished. Maybe some day I will succeed with sugar and chocolate.

February 2

Change is coming and I'm getting scared. The contractor has replaced the architect in meetings with Doug. That means the day of the ground breaking for the new building is getting closer. There are going to be things that aren't as good as the way it is now. I think. Now everybody eats at the same time in the same dining room. There's a lot of noise, but also a lot of merriment. It's the only time I get to see the north wing aides and nurses. While they're waiting for the trays to come out, we indulge in joke telling and bits of gossip or just horsing around. When the new building is built, there will be three dining rooms—one on the first floor, one on the second floor, and the present one made smaller for the seventeen residents who will be on the present south wing. In the new dining rooms we'll probably have two aides and a nurse. That's all.

Another thing I'm going to miss: on weekends I sit in the lobby in the morning and chat with the receptionist. I often call the kitchen and ask them to bring me some coffee. Since the kitchen is only about twenty-five feet away from where I'm sitting, it's no big deal. And now, when I'm in the dining room playing cards, I can see what's going on in the adjacent activities room and often get a little entertainment from it. But when I'm in a different wing I won't be able to do those things.

There's going to be advantages, of course. The resident rooms will be larger, and it will be nice to have just one other person living in the room. And the heating and cooling system will be newer. But I'm afraid much of the intimacy will be gone. I'm sure there will be minuses and pluses that are unpredictable from my present vantage point. I hope the pluses will outnumber the minuses, but I admit I'm scared. Change is always a bit frightening. And things aren't too bad the way they are now.

I never thought of nursing homes until I came to one, but if I had thought of them I would have pictured them as quiet, dull places with people lying in beds and slumped in wheelchairs waiting to die. Part of that is true. Some are lying in bed because they're too ill to sit up, and some are slumped in wheelchairs. But, in general, nursing homes are lively places, made so mostly by the staff, most of whom are under forty.

(This is not to imply that those over forty are not lively. Just wait until that salesman brings my motorized wheels!) I have come to think of many of the staff as my extended family.

I said in the prologue that it was traumatic when I had to go into a wheelchair. Later I found out that not being able to walk was not a big deal. It was being unable to transfer myself that shrunk my world. It would be great to be able to travel like many of my friends do. But that was not to be for me.

So yes, change is hard. And scary. And often unwanted. But I think the process of growing elderly alone is worse. Many people are afraid of nursing homes and are afraid they will end up where they least want to be. I am glad I could come while I still had my faculties about me to make it my home. When I think of the isolation and boredom I would have endured had I avoided this decision, I shudder. Instead, I am thankful that I made the change that brought me here and enriched my life with so many friends.

There's a lot to be said, too, for a lifestyle that sees your dirty breakfast, lunch and dinner dishes carried into a kitchen in which you never have to set foot. And that's really a good thing because the disappearance of the numbness in my foot was a fluke. Both my feet have been partially numb for some time now. I fear this will lead to amputation some day. Oh well. That's one way to get rid of these football clodhopper shoes.

I want to acknowledge how proud I am of my daughter Kathy and her husband John, who made each other promise to put the other in a nursing home if the care ever became too burdensome. They'll have to carry on the hilarity and entertainment for me. Lord knows I won't be hanging around in this world forever.

But wherever I am at that point, I expect I'll be having fun.

Epilogue

A Note from Peggy:

I WAS FIVE YEARS OLD when Mom noticed her first MS symptoms. When I was in elementary school, she would hold my arm to steady herself as we walked. I didn't mind it so much, but my next two older sisters were at ages where they would have been embarrassed if their friends had seen them holding their mother's hand. I guess I had an advantage of being so young when Mom got MS.

Since I was always the first one home from school, I learned to cook at an early age. Mom, cushioned with towels and a donut on her chair in the living room, would yell out each step that I had to take to get dinner ready. She was always very specific. "Put a pinch of salt in the potatoes," she would say, and then she'd tell me to look at her fingers making the motion of what a pinch of salt should look like. Or, "Put the roast in the oven at 355 degrees," and then she'd ask me later if it was exactly 355 degrees. I got tired of the strict directions, so the first time I made rice and she told me to use two cups of water and one cup of rice, I filled the pan with what *looked* like two cups of water and then threw in one cup of rice. When the rice wasn't ready in time, she gave me a knowing smile and said, "You didn't measure the water, did you?" I guess Mom knew what she was doing after all.

I was in high school when Mom needed a wheelchair. It was emotionally hard for all of us, but maybe mostly for Dad.

One of his customers told him about a spiritual healer by the name of Kathryn Kuhlman. When Kuhlman came to Buffalo, Dad took Mom to the meeting, expecting Mom to be healed. I don't think Mom was expecting healing though. Her philosophy was to avoid expecting good results. That way you didn't become disempowered if you didn't get what you wanted.

Mom came home that night with the same symptoms as always, but Dad no longer had arthritis and hernia pain. That made Mom wonder why God would fail to notice her. And Dad made things worse when he accused Mom of not receiving healing because she lacked faith. They attended Kuhlman's meetings in Pittsburgh a few times more. A couple of those times Susan and I accompanied them. I felt uncomfortable because I was afraid I'd make a scene with some sort of healing, like a lot of people did there. I think Mom felt that way too, even though she never said it.

Though I loved both of my parents, I had more compassion for Mom. Dad yelled at her a lot. After all, it was hard taking care of someone who needed to be lifted into a wheelchair and onto a toilet four times a day. She needed to be waited on all the time. Dad built a ramp up the steps in the garage so Mom could get out of the house and go places with us. I loved having her come along with us, but I will admit that it was a lot of work.

I came home from my first year at college to find that our baby grand piano had been sold. We needed room for a hospital bed in that corner of the living room. Mom slept in the living room, and Dad got her a bedpan to keep on the table next to her. That way she could use it when no one was home to take her to the bathroom. The first person home would empty it.

I worked at a nursing home during the summer after my first year of college—the same nursing home where Mom eventually lived. I thought I wanted to be a nurse. Since my shift was from 7:00 a.m. to 3:00 p.m., I always arrived home before anyone else. I came home one day, after showering people and emptying their bedpans all day, and Mom's first words were, "Will you empty my bedpan?" I decided, in that moment, that I would no longer seek a nursing career. I didn't want to spend the rest of my life waiting on people. And I didn't want my weariness of doing menial tasks for people to spill over onto Mom. It gave me empathy for the nurse's aides that took care of Mom all those years and did it with a happy heart.

During a typical morning in the later years that Mom lived with us at home, we would give her a piece of fruit for breakfast and some more fruit and celery for lunch later on. We always made sure her water glass was full. She would lie in bed and watch TV, read, or sleep. When someone came home she would usually greet him or her with a pleasant hello followed by, "Will you empty my bedpan?" Often, the first person home would then take her to the toilet. A visiting nurse taught Dad and me how to lift her without hurting ourselves. We would bounce her saying, "one, two, three," and on "three," we would lift up and she would push up as much as she could.

One time I was getting her off the toilet, and we must have had a little more energy than usual. We flew up and I fell over backward, into the bathtub. Mom was on top of me when the shower curtain came falling down. We both started laughing, but we didn't know what to do. Luckily, Dad had come home, and he heard the loud thud when I hit the bathtub. Not knowing what to expect, he opened the bathroom door to find Mom's tush sticking out from under the shower curtain and my legs dangling beneath.

Though such happenings gave us laughter, there generally wasn't much to laugh about. Mom had an existence without hope. One time she was feeling so distraught that I walked through the front door, and, instead of asking me to empty her bedpan, she asked me for a razor blade. I loved Mom, and I hated that she hated life.

I was scared when she talked about moving to a nursing home. It seemed so final. I had since moved to Pennsylvania and wasn't available to help anymore. Mom and Dad had a college student living with them who helped Dad with cooking, cleaning, and taking care of Mom. So I felt that my opinion wasn't worth much. And I mostly kept it to myself.

I lived only two hours away, so I drove up to visit about once every month. When I first saw Mom at Amherst Nursing Home, she seemed scared but happier than at home. I smiled a lot and pretended to be happy for her. At about my third visit with her, she no longer seemed scared. She had made some friends. I think the African violet fiasco made her feel as though she had taken ownership of her new home. And I was relieved that she had the level of care she required. I knew that I could not take care of her for the rest of her life, though I had considered it. It had been a very difficult decision for me to move out of town. But now that she had all her physical needs met, as well as much of her social and emotional needs, I was able to let go of a guilt that had overwhelmed me sometimes. Coworkers and acquaintances would say to me, "I could never put *my* mother in a nursing home." I accepted that they looked down on me, and I actually looked down on them, too.

During Mom's seventies she seemed to handle change well. But as she got older, she became more resistant to new things. Her fear of moving to the new building seemed to bother her more than it would have previously. But when she got to the new building, she loved it. The room was smaller, but she only had one roommate—and I never heard her complain about her roommate. The activities room, where she played cards, was smaller too, but the TV was there, inviting companionship with not only her card-playing friends but others as well. The nurses' station was central to all hallways. When I visited, this area was usually where I would find her, chatting with anyone who passed her way. The building stayed cooler, too, since they piped water through the ceilings and walls to help keep the temperature consistent.

Dad's death meant that Mom no longer had family living in Buffalo. But she made friends easily. Rosalia looked after her as she would her own mother. She or Rhonda visited Mom nearly every day, and Mom's nurse kept my sisters and me up to date. When her health began to decline in 2008, Kathy and I were able to visit her early that October. But even when we couldn't be there, the nurses could—they attended to her physical needs as well as gave her emotional comfort. When she died in late November, she was among people who loved her, and whom she loved in return.

I am grateful for her friends at Elderwood. They gave her joy. And when I think about it, I can see that her life was much more fulfilling there than it would have been if I had stayed in Buffalo and taken care of her myself. She always had someone to hold her hand when she needed it. And she laughed much.

Notes

1. p. 146.

2. Several authors have been credited with this poem. The *Northwestern Christian Advocate* July 13, 1904, credits Rev. Luther F. Beecher (1813–1903) as the author of this version.